The Music Script in Film

Conrado Xalabarder

The Music Script in Film © Conrado Xalabarder, 2013.
All rights reserved.
No part of this book may be used or reproduced in any manner whatsoever without written permission from the author, except in the case of brief quotations embodied in critical articles and reviews.

Translation from the Spanish: Gloria Montero

Front Cover Design:
typewriter photo © mediagram - Fotolia.com
cover concept: Conrado Xalabarder
sketches: Pablo Laspra and Óscar Araujo
score: Marc Vaíllo. "el habitante incierto" (Guillem Morales, 2005)
cover and back cover final design: Marcos Xalabarder

Registers:
Intellectual Property: B-4420-12
Safe Creative: 1311189363107

ISBN-13: 978-1494253356
ISBN-10: 1494253356

Visit www.mundobso.com

The composer who does not propose solutions is one who simply follows instructions.

Dedicated to all the composers who are script-writers and filmmakers, and to all the directors, producers and mixers who are not afraid of music and who respect the work of the composers.

This book is meant to be a point of departure, not a destination.

Contents

1. Introduction 7
2. The Domain of Music in Film 13
3. Categories of Music 23

    3.1. By Origin 23
    3.2. By Application 29
    3.3. By What it Communicates 39
    3.4. By Attitude 41
    3.5. By Allocation 44
    3.6. By Connection 47
    3.7. The Impossible Timing 54

4. Levels of Music 57

    4.1. Perceptive and Sonorous 57
    4.2. Narrative 63
    4.3. Spatial 65
    4.4. Dramatic 71

5. Distribution of Music 77

    5.1. Film scores with a thematic structure 78
    - Central themes 79
    - Main theme 83
    - Counter-theme 89
    - Secondary themes 96
    - Initial theme 97
    - Final theme 103
    - Sub-theme 107
    - Fragments and motifs: the leit-motif 109
    - Progression of themes 112

    5.2. Film scores without a thematic structure 118
    5.3. Songs 122

6. The Music Script 125

    6.1. How much music? 126
    6.2. What kind of music? 128
    6.3. For what purpose and for whom? 133
    6.4. Musical silence 143
    6.5. How, where and why? 144
    6.6. Music and dialogue 146
    6.7. Music and film sequences 150
    6.8. When should the music be written? 156

7. Final Words 163

8. Aforementioned Films 165

1. Introduction: The Power of Music

«I hate music in pictures… I don't like to see a man alone in the desert, dying of thirst, with the Philadelphia Orchestra behind him».[1]

John Ford

The above was said by one of the most famous directors in film history. It must be remembered that all pictures he made since the appearance of sound have been accompanied by music, in many cases written by first-class composers. Ford was not the only one to make known his dislike of music in film and it is not unusual to hear criticism from diverse sectors about music being used as if it were an element not only inconvenient and unnecessary but also something imposed.

The most frequent argument against music in film is based on the accusation that it is a manipulative element conditioning the spectator, putting him in a passive position in front of the picture without much margin to react. Although these arguments could be qualified they are significant and fortunately true: the music is there exactly for that reason, to manipulate. But film itself manipulates space, time and emotions… cinema is a great lie and the music takes an active part in this lie. If the editing –which constructs the film's narration– participates as an active element in this manipulation of time and space, why shouldn't music be part of it as well? If we believe that the great Peter Ustinov is the Emperor Nero in *Quo Vadis* (Mervyn LeRoy, 1951) why shouldn't we believe that the equally great music by Miklós Rózsa is just the kind of music that was heard in that period, even if it wasn't? And what about *Planet of the Apes* (Franklin J. Schaffner, 1968)? Is it valid to submerge the spectator in

---

[1] CD «Cheyenne Autumn» (Label X LXCD 4, 1987)

a world that is completely invented? And if it is (and it certainly is!), why shouldn't music be able to participate in this invention?

It is important to take into account that in the real world, the world where we live our daily lives, music *per se* does not exist. We don't go around accompanied by beautiful melodies nor are our concerns reinforced by serious music. In the real world we choose the music that we want in our space, either by playing it ourselves, or by accepting what others may play. For instance, if we like the music that we hear from another room we may decide to allow it to invade our personal space or go somewhere else (a public place, a concert) where they play music we like. On the other hand, if our personal space is invaded by music we do not like, we either protest or are forced to suffer it if there is no other option. Even in a public space where we do not like the music, we don't waste time in leaving or, again, putting up with it if we are unable to leave. In any one of these options, the existence of music is a choice. Furthermore, unwelcome music, which invades our personal space, offends us considerably more than children's screams or the barking of dogs. Children and dogs are inevitable in the world (at least to a certain point) and we might presume they will eventually be quiet.

In movie theatres, when the lights go out and the film begins, real life goes on hold until the movie ends and the lights are turned on again. And if, in this period, we like the music that we hear, all is well. But if we don't like it, that's alright, too. We might begin to feel uncomfortable or troubled but would probably not leave...after all we don't usually go to a movie theatre just for the music! In real life, we are active subjects and, as such, we can defend ourselves from the music by walking out or by turning it off. In the cinema, where we are passive subjects, we can't do that. Whereas in real life we control the influence that music has on us, in a cinema the music controls us. This is part of its power.

We must remember one important thing in music—and not only in film music. Different from other arts, music does not lie *per se* but can be employed to falsify or to alter the perception of reality. Painting, sculpture, literature and cinema itself can tell us a pack of lies: a portrait that beautifies someone who is not attractive or a story that praises the heroics of a coward could be considered to have

1. Introduction: The Power of Music

altered reality. With music this is not possible. By itself, music does not have this same capacity and, even though it might pretend to have such power, it could never pull it off. Music always explains a truth... that of the composer. Though to the ears of an audience it may seem exaggerated or pompous, music always remains a truth. What is it then that it does in a film when, for instance, it takes part in tricking us into believing that a character is trustworthy when in fact he isn't? The answer lies in the way it is applied. Music plays the role of a kind of invisible curtain that allows the vision of an image, or the perception or information about a character to be altered. But of itself the music does not lie.

It works like a mathematical equation: by applying bucolic music to a beautiful landscape, the spectator will see a landscape that is even more beautiful. But if the music is disturbing, the landscape will no longer look beautiful but will alert to something terrible that is going to happen. On the other hand, a scene of hell is even more hellish with hellish music, but with a waltz the spectator will not feel the heat of the flames and will inevitably try to find beauty in the horror. And, in fact, he will no doubt find it because, if he does not, the music would make no sense.

Music allows us to alter the vision and the perception of reality (e.g. a beautiful landscape) but, in itself, does nothing to deceive. What is deceiving us is the film as a whole. Proof of this is that if we disassociate the music from the image and listen to it apart, we will find no deception in it at all. We will simply hear the music. This is part of its power. It adds a new dimension through a process somewhat like an optical illusion. The music, therefore, while not manipulative in itself, participates in the manipulation through what the film is narrating or what the images themselves are showing. It may well be said that the ideal would be for everything to be expressed visually through the dialogue and action and that, the less need to recur to music, so much the better for the film. This is something about which I am convinced—in film, less music usually can be considered more. Too often, excessive use of music either overloads or even takes away from the music's efficacy, something that is really important. In any case, for reasons that I will point out in this book, film almost always needs music to explain it. There are, of course, magnificent films that do not require even a second of music and function perfectly well without it. It all depends on what the picture needs music to cover.

In general, one tends to think that the communication between the music and the viewer is emotional and that this is linked with the images. While this is true enough, it is incomplete. Naturally, there is an emotional communication between the music and the viewer but there is also an intellectual communication where the music not only transmits emotion but the information necessary to properly comprehend scenes or characters, as well. In other words, the music is not only linked to the images. It is connected just as much to the literary film script, dealing with the narrative elements that sometimes are not even described there. It is quite normal that in a film there exist two scripts side by side—the literary and the music script— which on occasion move synchronistically, or perhaps asynchronistically, in the same direction while, at other times, in quite opposite directions. If this happens, what the music explains will be the dominant message because the viewer will find it difficult to question what it says. It will not matter how many trees and green fields are shown if what is heard is apocalyptic music. The music will always win.

Why is this so? Basically, because music is an element that, for the audience, appears to be merely sonorous and intangible, when in reality it can become visual and completely tangible, even somewhat physical. And because the audience does not perceive it in this way they are not able to explain it away and, therefore, are not able to control it, and in not controlling it, they are at its mercy, they do not question it. It goes without saying that in a well-made film nothing could be worse or more devastating for the film and its narrative discourse than to have its music questioned by the audience.

Music can play many roles. It can replace dialogue, express a character's feelings and even add what the words do not express. It can enter into the feelings or the psychology of a character and lay him or her bare before the spectator. A pleasant melody applied to someone will add a positive sensation. If what is heard produces anxiety, the information conveyed (and this without words) is that there are problems ahead. This is what happens when no tricks are used and the director is not using music to confuse the viewer, although at times this, too, can be useful. In the same way, a composer is able to define something with a few notes or with a melody. You have only to listen to the music in *Jaws* (Steven Spielberg, 1975), *The Omen* (Richard Donner, 1976) or *Close Encounters of the Third Kind* (Stephen Spielberg, 1977) where the shark, Satan and creatures from outer space are identified even when they are not seen. In these cases, the music enters into an intellectual communication with the audience, linked not only with the image but with the storyline as well. However, not only is music able to define people, animals or creatures from outer space but also concepts such as love, war and horror. It can be used to either express something in the film or to condition the vision of the viewer, either in a subtle specific way or quite frankly, in a manner that is easy to interpret.

If music is used in a film, it is because it is needed: either to solve concrete problems, to strengthen the narrative discourse or to construct an alternative storyline. A composer who wants to work in an audiovisual medium must understand these needs and satisfy them. It is not enough to know how to write music (one assumes a composer already knows this). A film composer must be able to construct a musical discourse, control the rhythm, sacrifice what is merely tempting for the benefit of what is necessary and thus become the film's music scriptwriter. The composer who knows only how to put melodic music to a pretty landscape will only ever be called upon to do exactly that. At a much more significant level, the composer who is able to change the way a scene is viewed or a character understood will be contracted in both these cases. However, at a really essential level, the composer who knows how to write a music script will stop being a mere composer to become a scriptwriter and be able to add music at any of the three levels and, even more important, to offer solutions that will benefit the film as a whole.

One thing should never be forgotten. *The composer who does not propose solutions is one who simply follows instructions.* If you are a composer, the aim of this book is to help convert you into a filmmaker. And if you are a filmmaker, it aims to help you write a music script which you can give to the composer so that it can be returned to you in the form of music. In either case, both composer and director will be making the film together.

1. Introduction: The Power of Music

Writing a music script demands order. Think of it in chess terms. Nobody wins a game of chess by following emotional rather than rational impulses. In the same way, to write a music script, you need to know how to deal adequately with the elements at your disposal which should not be moved emotionally but with clear-headed reason. As a result, the emotion will inevitably be much better expressed, because constructing a music script is almost identical to playing a game of chess.

Conrado Xalabarder, 2013

2. The Domain of Music in Film

If we were to ask most movie-goers what makes for a good soundtrack, the overwhelming majority would probably say "one with good music". That would certainly be the response of some composers who write film music. However, this is not always the case.

Can we consider film music good when, while impeccably written and performed, it fails to do what it has been assigned? Is it good when it is expected to bring about a specific reaction and, for whatever reason, fails to do so? Can it be said to be good when it confuses rather than clarifies? Or when it fails to add the information needed?

One thing is *good music* while *good film music* is something quite different. They are not the same thing. If we judge film music as good or bad by strictly musical criteria, we will classify it by its musical qualities, simply as music. Is it well written or performed? This type of judgment is not necessarily subjective nor does it take into account different genres or styles in music. We are talking here of evaluating any music from a purely musical point of view. It would make no sense to compare Baroque music and jazz because they are quite different styles but we could compare two pieces of Baroque music. This is usually the same criteria used when evaluating the quality of music written for film but it does not make sense. While romantic music for film may be compared with the romantic music of any classical composer, such a comparison is entirely out of place.

A good film composer is not one who writes the best music but one who adds music that is of greatest value to the film. The criteria for such value refers to what the music is supposed to do and the result it brings to the film. Does it work or not? In horror films, does the music provoke fear? In a romantic film, does it arouse the emotions or leave the spectator indifferent? Does it help resolve the needs of the film or is it a hindrance? Does it clarify where clarification is needed or does it confuse? In overall terms, is the music useful? This shows up the enormous difference between music for film and other types of music and is the principal way it should be evaluated. Good film music is that which is useful to the movie, and this must be the composer's objective. From this it is easy to see how 'bad' music (considered purely from the criteria of musical quality) may well be great film music or that a fine score may be considered 'bad' from a cinematic point of view. A musical composition may be splendid for the concert hall but poorly suited to a film. What is the use of trying to describe a person by means of a musical theme if the spectator cannot link the theme with the character?

It is not necessary to sacrifice musical quality in order to achieve the maximum usefulness of music in film. The main requirement is efficiency: 'good' music is simply not enough. Of course, there may be cases where the music is neither good in quality nor in usefulness. In other words, as well as being poor musically, it fails to serve the interests or needs of the film. Normally, what we hear are fine creations that are also valid for the movie, when a composer writes a good musical score that is useful because he/she knows how to make it fit the needs of the film for which it was created. Can 'bad' music actually be 'good' in cinematic terms? Where this is the case, it obviously plays a positive role. However, you might well ask if this music, being useful, might be even better if it were also 'good'? Not necessarily. A movie may need that the music be really 'bad' or badly performed, which does not mean that a bad composer be contracted to write it. In *Citizen Kane* (Orson Welles, 1941), with music by Bernard Herrmann, one of the characters is a mediocre young performer who aspires to become an opera singer and whose all-powerful lover financially backs the launching of a work aimed at making her a great success. Herrmann wrote an aria, *Salamboo*, the work she had to sing. The script specified that the reviews were to be negative in every respect; the aria had to be very poorly sung and sound dreadful. Otherwise the audience might approve a rendition that was supposed to be horrendous. Herrmann did not write 'bad' music, he simply wrote it to sound appalling.

If a character in a movie is playing a violinist with little talent, it would not make sense for him/her to perform brilliantly. On the other hand, it would add something to see the violinist playing the instrument badly. For *The Man with the Golden Arm* (Otto Preminger, 1955), Elmer Bernstein wrote the music Frank Sinatra played (jazz percussion) as he underwent a down-hill trip because of his addiction to drugs. This clearly underlined the point and helped us understand the agony he was suffering. Here we are able to discriminate between two characters, providing one with good music as opposed to another whose music is vulgar. However, starting out with 'bad' music (without any need to *make it worse* for dramatic purposes) may also turn out to be effective. For example, in order to recreate an ugly, vulgar and decadent atmosphere there could be nothing better than to apply 'bad' music.

At its highest level of usefulness to a film, music becomes more than just music, it becomes pure cinema. Because of this, it is important to be able to distinguish between the *what, why and how* of its use. We shall deal with this later but for now let us consider a representative example of how music may come to have more visual than musical importance, namely the sequence with the shower in *Psycho* (Alfred Hitchcock, 1960). What did Bernard Herrmann do to make this scene so powerful?

When Hitchcock finished shooting this film he felt dissatisfied and decided to re-edit it in order to have it included in the television series *Alfred Hitchcock Presents,* which at that time had a huge following. Nevertheless, Herrmann suggested Hithcock might take a holiday to give him time to write a score that could solve the problems troubling the director. Hitchcock agreed but gave him precise instructions. He did not want to hear a single note in the shower sequence. Herrmann took no notice and for this scene composed a theme that ended up becoming one of the grand references in cinema. When the director saw it, he was not only enthusiastic about its powerful effect but now it had this theme he decided to release the film.

This scene has been widely written about in efforts to analyze the reasons for its impact and also the intentions of the composer who limited himself to defining his goal in a one word—*terror*. One of the interpretations makes reference to the onomatopoeia of the birds, which Norman Bates (the central character) collects stuffed, as if it were these that were attacking the victim. The constant and obsessive sound of the squealing violins and the fact that soon after Hitchcock would direct *The Birds* (1963) support this theory. Another view points to the possibility that these sounds are repeating the desperate screams of pain from Marion Crane (the victim), which would put the music in the epicenter of tension. A third theory, and the one that in my judgment comes closest to reality, is that which maintains that the violins emulate Bates' stabbing of the woman who, in fact, is not seen being stabbed at all. Indeed, if we watch the sequence, we see that no flesh is cut, which adds further to the viewer's confusion.

In the author's opinion, the reality is simpler and because of this more brilliant. Marion Crane suffers nine stabs which the spectator perceives visually. With the hysterical violins, Bernard Herrmann offers the spectator a total of fifty stabs. This implies that while we are seeing the nine stabs what we seem to observe, psychologically and emotionally, are fifty savage attacks. If Herrmann had matched the violins to these attacks, the sequence would not have had any effect. But having created an unreal situation, what it generates is a state of total chaos provoked by the brutal break between visual and sound perception.

The music does not follow the images but runs independently so that for a brief period of time the spectator must deal with two opposing dramatic effects—one visual and the other of sound. This chaos lasts only a short time but seems to go on forever in the unconsciousness of a witness to the killing. Furthermore, in order to prevent the spectator from reacting, the rhythm, while maintained, changes chaotically, multiplying the sensation of disorder and consequently of terror. As a result, it is easy to understand that, when he saw it with this new theme, Hitchcock was prepared to release the movie, which became his greatest box-office success. Herrmann, we might say, made use of visual music.

Think about that music. Do you feel it would bring an ovation from the public in concert halls used to listening to Mozart, Bach or Beethoven? I doubt it. The theme is extremely simple. But who could outdo its effect? Naturally, what Herrmann wrote was music, but more than that he was making a film. For the same reason, we should understand that the real intention of the uncomfortable and even disagreeable music written by the duo Trent Reznor and Atticus Ross for *The Girl with the Dragon Tattoo* (David Fincher, 2011), what Hans Zimmer wrote for *The Dark Knight Rises* (Christopher Nolan, 2012) or Roque Baños for *Evil Dead* (Fede Álvarez, 2013) lies in the films themselves.

One question often raised challenges the validity of film music outside the cinema—in recordings or in concert halls. That is, outside its natural surroundings. While it is not entirely incorrect to say that film music, when separated from its celluloid base, loses part of its meaning. It does need to be qualified. First of all, it is true that the place of music written for film is in the film. Composers know this although there are some who take advantage of the medium to promote themselves quite apart from any cinematographic concerns. In any case, it is significant that when a writer works for film his output is called a *script* and as such it cannot be compared with a novel although the business of writing is the same (only the technique is different). But the composer is not able, unjustly perhaps, to avoid a comparative evaluation, despite his not working in the same medium. This leaves open to discussion whether there really exists a musical form that may be called *cinematographic*. In his book "La musique au Cinéma", Michel Chion states that *"there does not exist a truly film music style. This music draws on all possible sources in just the same way as does a composer of concert or opera music. The difference lies in the fact that, in principal, the latter is free to create his own personal style, not only starting out from what he invents but also from what he takes from others"*.[2] What Chion does is make a strictly musical analysis and from this perspective his statement is valid. In any case, the most important point is to insist that when music goes beyond the musical and moves into visual territory it then turns into something unique. Naturally, it continues to be music but it becomes something different. This is because it depends on its own narrative structures which, while perhaps very close to opera, have qualities quite specific to the audiovisual media where music can be used, for

---

[2] "Il n'existe pas à propement parler de style de musique de film. Celle-ci prend son bien partout, à l'instar, d'a illeurs d'un compositeur de musique de concert ou d'opéra. La différence est que ce dernier a tout loisir, en principle, de créer son style personnel, non seulement à partir de ce qu'il invente mais aussi de ce qu'il prend aus autres". Chion, M. «La musique au Cinéma» (Fayard, 1995). P. 248.

instance, to create an extreme close-up during a wide-shot. Just as a novelist has to change his/her technique and even style to write film scripts, the same is true of a composer. For this reason, because music for film requires a specific technique, it must be considered an entirely different genre although, it must be said that, as such, there is no definitive cinematographic style.

In any case, composers naturally aim at obtaining the maximum benefit from their efforts. Once their immediate task is completed, must they accept that their work will be known only from the film? Not at all. When the composer gives up those elements involving motivation and application, including the very concept of genre, he or she accepts that their work be evaluated from an objective perspective (the *what*). For instance, in a concert of film music, the composer must be open to being compared with other composers whose music is only played in concert halls.

Another matter is that related to contemporary works applied to silent films. Clearly, anyone can take a film and compose, according to his/her inspiration, a piece of music. However, this does not make it the *soundtrack* of a film given that it is purely an interpretation. Putting music to silent film has occasionally become an opportunity for some musicians to shine as they are able to work under optimum conditions without having to take into consideration anyone's arguments but their own. Sometimes the result is brilliant, while at others, it falls short.

When we examine music for film from a purely musical perspective (the *what*), we make a rigorous analysis of the music itself. But this is not enough. Concert music, for example, is in principal a voluntary act of creation that needs no justification. In film, on the other hand, justification rules everything. Applied music must have a clear reason for its presence, otherwise it would not make sense. A beautiful waltz applied to an apocalyptical sequence would have to be justified or it would be quite unacceptable. This is the big difference between good film music and what might be termed simply music for film. And shows why we cannot compare the music of a concert hall composer with that of a composer for film. The vehicle of expression (music) is the same but the fields of action (the concert hall and the wide screen) are completely different. The film composer has a double task. On the one hand he/she has to write the music but at the same time the work must make sense in cinematographic terms. This can be done without sacrificing musical ideas or convictions, although at times the sacrifice may be necessary for the good of the film. Later on, we shall deal with the third element characteristic of film music which is the form that is applied (the *how*) which is also very important.

Music is a human creation that expresses human emotions and when applied to film, incorporates that dimension and transmits it to the spectator. However, it can go even further. Think what happens in animation or in films and documentaries about the animal world. When animation represents humans there is the possibility that they will appear simply as schematic or made-up representations of persons. However, when music is applied to them as if they were real people, this helps to humanize them. In the case of animals this is even more evident. There is no music in the animal world. Animals do not live, hunt or feel through music but, when music is applied to them, human emotions and sentiments are attributed to them which the spectator also experiences. It is one of the many licenses one may take with music and, furthermore, it is something that is accepted and never questioned. In exactly the same way, music may also be applied to imaginary beasts, people from other planets or even machines. Applying music to anything at all serves to humanize or at least to attribute understandable emotions to whatever it might be.

There are limits, however, to what music can do. When one attempts to go beyond the limit and is unsuccessful, an effect opposite to that desired may well be provoked. What music is there in drinking a glass of milk or eating an orange? There is no music that can explain these actions. Nevertheless, we can apply *music of thirst or hunger*, even that *of pleasure* or any other emotional reaction that might result from drinking a glass of milk or eating an orange. However, the act in itself, the eating and drinking cannot be explained with music because these are biological processes. In much the same way we might ask what music could be put to a rape? None at all for the act itself. We could put music from the perspective of the rapist (contempt, cruelty) or of the victim (humiliation, suffering) or we could make the spectator a participant (violence), but it would be difficult to find music that would explain or put the spectator at a level with the act—

savage and inhuman—of rape. This is certainly true if we wanted to explain the rape itself and not the reactions it provokes. In *Schindler's List* (Steven Spielberg, 1993), whatever music were to be added with the intention of matching the horror and depravity of the Nazis and the Holocaust would inevitably be inadequate and could even trivialize it. One can not expect to explain something inacceptable and inexplicable with music. For this reason, not a single note of John Williams' music was devoted to this task.

What music, in any strict sense, could be applied to a zombie? Absolutely none if they are treated as zombies, simply chunks of flesh without soul or spirit. Putting music over them would humanize them and give them feelings they do not have and, furthermore, to give them these feelings would provide the hope of their becoming human again, which would be nothing short of cruel. It may seem frivolous to talk about zombies (who used to be human), but it is interesting to see how they have been treated in many films. Generally, they are backed by scary music aimed at reinforcing the sensation of danger felt by the spectator and the other film characters rather than describing the zombies themselves. In fact, if we were to apply violin music to a zombie, the viewer would automatically feel that the zombie had not yet lost his soul or spirit. In the highly successful television series *The Walking Dead* (2010), Bear McCreary's music—other than that applied to the humans—is aimed at creating feelings of anxiety although there is a very interesting episode in the second season. In it, the characters, who have discovered that a large number of zombies have been locked in a stable, open the doors to let them out and then carry out a massive slaughter. This whole sequence is accompanied by beautiful dramatic music that is intensely tormented. It expresses the pain and confusion of one of the humans who had locked them up with the hope of one day recovering them when science made this possible. This same music is also laid in over the zombies and suddenly these are turned into humans, and are no longer mere chunks of walking flesh. By humanizing them it is easier to sympathize with them. Zombies, however, like a stone or a glass of milk or a rape, do not have music of themselves. Neither do men or women, gay or straight people. We must maintain control of the limits that must not be crossed when we are dealing with them or else the situation will appear trite. We must also know how to use the absence of music so that it ends up having a musical value.

At this point, everything becomes a question of choice, of deciding how we want the spectator to view a sequence. For example, imagine a scene where a couple is having sex in the intimacy of a room. Depending on the music we apply we shall see different stories emerging from the same images. If the music is romantic, we shall see a couple in love. If the music is hot and sensual (with a saxophone, a most sensual instrument) we shall see carnal desire. Depending on how intense the music is, this desire will seem to be of greater or lesser intensity. If we lay in very dramatic music, we may well feel they are taking advantage of their last chance because the end of the world is near! What happens if we add no music? We turn it into a purely biological act, a copulation as animal-like as drinking milk or eating an orange. We do not have to change the scene in the slightest, either in the editing or in its choreography. Simply by applying any one of these musical options we decide how the scene should be seen and understood by the spectator. We do not even need the help of dialogue to tell us if they love each other, desire each other or fear the coming of a catastrophic meteorite. The music does it all. And this makes up an essential part of its power.

The objective is not only to resolve a scene one way or another, to decide how to audience should see and interpret it, but to arrive at an overall construct that makes sense and is logical. It must not leave any loose ends and, perhaps most important of all, what we want to say with the music must be understood. For this purpose, it is not enough to be enthusiastic and willing. Emotion does not create a music script. As mentioned earlier, no one wins a game of chess simply with passion. We must know how to work out a strategy, calculate the effects to be obtained with each move and, above all, know thoroughly the resources available to achieve the desired result.[3]

---

[3] In his book «The Emerging Film Composer» (Amazon, 2006. P. 68) author Richard Bellis gives a useful advice to newcomers: "The tendency of film music students is to write their impression of the scene. When this happens, they are merely reiterating what the scene is already saying. We rather should be diagnosing what the scene needs to be saying and is not. If the scene is complete without music then there should be no music. This is what is meant by servicing the film. When you merely write your impression of the film, you are usurping the film for your own creative methods".

2. The Domain of Music in Film

In other sections of this book, we shall deal with those resources which apply largely and specifically to the audiovisual media and make it possible for music to go beyond being simply *good* to being a *useful tool*. This is the domain of music for film.

3. Categories of Music

Music for film has its own characteristics, which make it a useful tool for both sound and visual narration. These combine, of course, with traditional and practical elements of musical composition, in general. Whether original or taken from other sources, music is used to construct the narrative story that results in the music script. To be fully aware of the reasons music is being used, the ways in which it is applied and the interrelation it establishes with the picture, it is essential to begin with basic theoretical definitions. In this chapter, we will set out those categories of music that are interrelated and how they need to be complemented by what is dealt with in following chapters. For this reason, no section in this book should be regarded as definitive without keeping in mind those still to come.

3.1. By origin: original, existing and adapted

In a soundtrack we may find a mix of original music, music expressly written for a film and existing music created earlier and not written for the film in hand (classical music, for example). As we shall see, making use of original music has many advantages and few drawbacks. On the other hand, as well as its virtues, the use of existing music holds certain risks. It often happens that existing music is used without taking these risks into account, especially when there are not as many factors justifying its inclusion.

Where a film deals with the life of a composer, it is logical to use his/her music. In *Amadeus* (Milos Forman, 1984) the soundtrack is made up of themes by Mozart, something that could not have been avoided. Where a film is set at an historical moment and we have to show the period, it is reasonable to make use of music of that time, although this should be done with care. Laying music by Haendel in a film set in the British court of the 18th century would make sense, but might not if the film, set in the same country and century, dealt exclusively with the life of rural folk. They probably would never have had a chance to ever hear Haendel! If a character has some special interest in a singer or well-known tune, it would not be out of place for a melody or the songs of this singer to be included, whether or not the character is listening to them or simply because it has been decided to emphasize this preference.

The reasons justifying the use of existing music are essentially those forming part of the argument, that is to say, what the film needs for setting its location, to understand a character, the historical context or some specific reference. This is the case, for example, with the music associated with the character of Bela Lugosi played by Martin Landau in *Ed Wood* (Tim Burton, 1994). In this film, a fragment of Tchaikovsky's *Swan Lake* was used because it was the main theme of the *Dracula* soundtrack (Tod Browning, 1932), the film that really launched Lugosi to stardom. It also underlined the old Hungarian actor's days of splendor now past, symbolizing the decline and failure that lies ahead of him and cannot be avoided.

Existing music can also be used when it is not apparently justified but serves to provide a deliberate contrast. This was the case in *2001: A Space Odyssey* (Stanley Kubrick, 1968) in which Strauss's *Blue Danube* was laid in over futuristic images. We see this in the case of the combination of songs and classical music that Sofia Coppola used in *Marie Antoinette* (2006) where songs accompanied the queen and classical Baroque the courtly scenes. However, if existing music has no clear justification in a film it runs three significant risks. The first risk is aesthetic, when applying this music without any story justification breaks the unity of style in the entire music script. In other words, this music has absolutely nothing to do with the other music in the film. The second risk lies in the narrative. When existing music is used it is taking a place that logically should be occupied by original music. When this happens, it may interrupt or even destroy the development of the theme taken out of its proper context. The result may prejudice the film and be disastrous for the music script. The third and most significant risk is the danger of distracting the attention of the viewer and this is the worst thing that could happen. A film cannot allow the audience to suddenly start wondering where the music was heard before, or perhaps start to hum it without paying attention to what it is narrating. If instead of *putting you* in the film, (the objective of original music and one of its real values when well done), it loses your attention and takes you away. This is a serious error usually provoked by directors who use music they like (music they feel the audience will like, too), even when it has nothing to do with the film and nearly always goes against the criteria of the composer.

An example that incorporates these three risks is found in the unfortunate music script of *The Elephant Man* (David Lynch, 1980), a film that tells the life of John Merrick, a young man who suffered from a terrible physical malformation and was displayed as an animal oddity in a circus. Finally, he was rescued by a doctor who put him in a hospital. The composer John Morris had drawn up an intelligent music script which was spoiled by the director's wrong decision in applying Samuel Barber's *Adagio for Strings* over the film's most significant dramatic sequence. This was when the main character, having carried out his humble day-to-day objectives and aware he had little time left, decided to end his life by sleeping lying down like other people and thus asphyxiating himself by the weight of his huge head. The composer's idea was to give the central character not just one but two themes—that of the animal (as others used to see him) and that of John Merrick, the human being hiding behind that physical horror. The central theme of *The Elephant Man*, started out full of power as the initial theme—music that included the idea of the circus, dramatic/melancholic in a muted tone, as if it were *music in black and white*. A brief fragment of this theme would be used in the scene when Doctor Trevis and a colleague are watching Merrick from a window, taking him back to the wagon which will return him to the circus.[4]

Later on, in another scene, while the guard makes the nightly rounds of the hospital that leads to his finding the protagonist in his room, we hear a dramatic variation that serves to open the way to this encounter. Another apparition comes in the humiliation scene which takes the form of a macabre ballet which we shall deal with in another chapter. After this, the theme will not be heard again until Merrick's

---

[4] The two speak about him and one asks what his mental state could be like. Doctor Trevis answers that medically he believes Merrick to be an imbecile (but not in the insulting sense of the word) and feels this to be the case. At that moment, because he sees him as an animal, we hear fragments from this theme.

complete destruction when he returns to London after being kidnapped and is followed by a huge crowd in Victoria Station. At this point, the composer applied a truncated version of the theme. As this was the end of Merrick's nightmare, it was a clever way to eliminate it.

John Merrick's central theme was to have come up three times. The first time was when Dr. Trevis and the hospital director, listening to him recite a poem, realized he was not mentally deficient. This theme was a poetic melody that underlined the dignity of the central character. When it came in a second time it had a bigger role in the sequence where, in his room, Merrick begins to construct a model of the cathedral. (When he finishes this is when he decides to put an end to his life). In theory, the poetic melody ought not to have been heard again (fully developed) until the scene where he decided it was time to stop his suffering and die. At this point, the central theme would emerge as the main theme, to substitute in power and relevance the theme of the beast. However, here David Lynch inserted the Barber *Adagio* thus leaving John Merrick's theme without any justification at all. With this greatly weakened, Lynch saw no other solution than to end the film with a muted version of the *elephant man* theme. In other words, the process of dignifying and humanizing Merrick had not served for anything. He ended up again an animal.

This broke the stylistic unity of the music in the film as it had little to do with what John Morris had prepared. We cannot deny the music's exquisite beauty but it had no connection with what had been constructed in the course of the film. Lynch had no way of knowing that some years later the *Adagio* would appear in *Platoon* (Oliver Stone, 1986), a highly-successful film with great music written by Georges Delerue. This was catastrophic for *The Elephant Man*. New generations of film-goers who saw Lynch's film, would inevitably exclaim when they got to the death scene: *"That's the music from Platoon!"* And the sequence, the most important in the film, thus lost all its dramatic power. Rather than *putting* the spectator right in the film, it *took him/her out.*[5]

---

[5] If David Lynch had made the Adagio John Merrick's theme right from the start, it would have been more logical and the story would have worked well so long as he did not later use the Elephant Man theme.

If in *2001: A Space Odyssey* the public recognizes the Strauss waltz, it is because it was thus intended, to create a contrast between futuristic images and popular classical music. On the other hand, when the public recognizes the music and this distracts attention from the film, something is not working. While Woody Allen's films are full of existing musical themes this is justified by linking them with the city of New York. Quentin Tarantino's soundtracks are also loaded with existing musical themes from other films but here too this has its justification, mainly aesthetical, and it is something the spectator happily accepts because it forms part of the essence of those films and the Tarantino style. In a saga or series of films that develop the same story or have the same character it is logical that we hear music from earlier films, as in the series that started with *Star Wars* (George Lucas, 1977) or in the James Bond films. Borrowing music or using references to existing films for those that in principle have nothing to do with the original are usually done as parody and are thus fully justified. Parody was not intended in the animated film *The Incredibles* (Brad Bird, 2004) with music by Michael Giacchino which, while completely original, sounded very much like the music John Barry wrote for the James Bond saga, although indeed it was meant to refer to the Bond films. There is also a very close reference to the music of the Venetian composer Antonio Vivaldi in the original music Georges Delerue wrote for *A Little Romance* (George Roy Hill, 1979), about young love that takes place in the city of canals.

The great virtue of original music is its ability to integrate many things. The viewer is not expecting it, does not know it, and therefore in principle it does not distract or disturb the attention (unless, of course, it is not up to the task and doesn't work well). In addition, original music has qualities that existing music lacks---flexibility in modulation and in its duration. With original music a composer can control precisely all the inflexions in a sequence, adding emphasis to certain moments, subtlety to others, raising or lowering the tone, etc. To sum up, original music can satisfy what the scene requires, taking into account its duration as well as the dialogue. On the other hand, existing music is inflexible, cannot be modulated and has a specific tempo which cannot be changed (unless one does something not very elegant, such as cutting it because it is longer than the picture sequence). If a scene is not planned in keeping with existing music it may be difficult to match with the same precision that original music can offer.[6] With original music we can make variations on a theme, extend or restrict it. We can reduce it to a motif or fragment and we are able to modulate it depending on the narrative needs of the film.

There are times when existing music can work well without any need to justify it, even at the cost of breaking stylistic unity. However, this only works as long as it does not spoil narrative continuity or distract the attention of the spectator. Over a serial killer, for example, we could put music by Bach, well-known to the audience, and let them know that this sinister person is refined, cultivated and sophisticated, without any need to explain this in the narrative script. It forms part of the immediacy we find in musical communication. If in a film we want to mark an end and come to a new start (a parenthesis or a scene that stands apart from the rest), then the stylistic differentiation must be optimal. In *Elizabeth* (Shekhar Kapur, 1988) with music by David Hirschfelder, Mozart's *Requiem* is laid in over the key sequence when the queen decides to renounce being a woman to convert herself into an institution. She cuts her hair, covers her face with heavy make-up and declares: *From now on, I am married to England*. This is such a special sequence in the film as a whole that Mozart's music contributed to give it the proper ceremonial tone, almost religious, and quite different from the dramatic tone used in the rest of the film. Once this scene was over the film ended with original music.[7] Something similar happens in *The King's Speech* (Tom Hooper, 2010). The most important scene in the film (the radio address by the king) is not accompanied by music by Alexandre Desplat (who wrote the music for the rest of the film) but by Beethoven's *Seventh Symphony*. This scene was given a special, quite different status, also ceremonial in nature, and showed a dramatic and narrative tone clearly distinct from the rest of the film, something that would have been impossible to do without this kind of treatment.

---

[6] The film composer is like a person in an obstacle race. He/she must juggle dialogue, phrasing, emphasis and all the factors needed for a scene. On the other hand, in its application to film, existing music can have a destructive linear form.

[7] While it has a fine result this example is not comparable to that mentioned with regard to The Elephant Man and its great sequence where we hear Samuel Barber's Adagio because in that film there is an original theme that has its logical conclusion in that sequence.

A recent example of the application of existing music that has raised much discussion was the use of the romantic theme Bernard Herrmann wrote for *Vertigo* (Alfred Hitchcock, 1958) that was used in *The Artist* (Michel Hazanavicius, 2011), which has original music by Ludovic Bource. In this famous French film, Herrmann's music was used in one of the most dramatic scenes, the attempted suicide. The music Bernard Herrmann wrote for the famous kissing scene with a circular tracking shot in Hitchcock's film was not exactly music for an ordinary love scene, but was a theme dealing with the desperate need for love and the overwhelming desire to keep loving the lost beloved. In Hazanavicius's film, the most tragic elements of that music are used which, removed from any connection with its original reference, works wonderfully. There was no falling into aesthetic and narrative risks because, as it was a film that evoked silent movies, it was logical that the music not be structured but rather be a succession of themes that kept resolving the sequences as they happened. This was exactly what happened in many of those silent films as they had no thematic structure. Furthermore, this theme does not take up space that could belong to other music. With regard to the third risk, the decision is somewhat more complicated because, when it comes to the scene in question, a died-in-the-wool cinema buff could start thinking more about *Vertigo* than in what is taking place in the sequence being shown. The music takes the spectator out of the movie instead of putting him in it.[8] In any case, even though existing music in itself is inflexible, cannot be modulated and has a limited duration, it is still possible to adapt it if the scene is not edited according to the rhythm and duration of the music. Of course, even if adapted, it still remains existing music and as such must be justified.

3.2. By application: diegetic and incidental. False diegesis.

There are two possible applications of music in film: diegetic and incidental (or extra-diegetic). Music in diegesis, coming from recognizable sources (a radio, musical equipment, instruments, etc.), is heard realistically by the characters in the film. It happens in a

---

[8] I believe that the music works well because its tragic quality is in line with what is being narrated and the film itself is filled with direct references to other classical films. In any case, this was not strictly necessary.

specific place and lasts for an exact length of time. In *Casablanca* (Michael Curtiz, 1943), the song *As Time Goes By* is played on the piano quite realistically (a man plays the piano and sings the song) in a specific place (Rick's café), and it lasts an exact amount of time (the time the character takes to perform it). Incidental music, as it comes from abstract rather than from natural sources, has no realistic meaning. The viewer does not recognize where it comes from and the characters do not hear it. (Where, for instance, does the music in the shower sequence of *Psycho* come from?). It comes in places that are not concrete but simply part of the general ambience—the psychology or the emotions of the characters—and its duration does not respond to exact criteria, but lasts just as long as is needed in each scene, sometimes breaking off and starting up again, sometimes even a long time later.

The field of spatial and dramatic action of the diegesis has limitations when compared with the possibilities of incidental music. Physically, diegetic music can only be put wherever it might be heard. Its space is limited (the music from a radio can only be heard by those near the apparatus). However, there are no limits to the space incidental music can occupy. And this marks the difference between both kinds of music. With diegetic music, if the character moves away from the source, he also moves away from the music. This does not happen with incidental music which can accompany him wherever he may go. Diegetic music fills the scene over which it is applied and it is impossible to either reduce or expand it. But incidental music can be reduced or expanded way beyond the visual field. And, it goes without saying, that while diegetic music has a finite duration—it will last until the record or the orchestra has finished—incidental music can go on indefinitely.

Imagine a sequence that takes place in a park on a sunny morning. Centre scene are two characters (the principal characters) seated on a bench, declaring their love. Nearby, children are playing, people are walking by and some old people are reading the newspaper. In the park there is a bandstand where an orchestra is playing romantic music. This music is obviously heard or listened to by the main characters, the children, those passing by and the old people. It fills the whole scene. Now imagine that we repeat the sequence with the only exception that there is no orchestra in the bandstand. If the same music sounds incidentally, it is not being heard or listened to now by the central characters, the children, those passing by or the older people. As we have the two principals declaring their love, it will be evident to the spectator that this music is referring exclusively to their sentiments. Thus, through its intention (expressing the couple's love), we obtain perfect music for the close-up within the whole scene, while at the same time it has changed from being environmental (that of an idyllic sunny morning) to become dramatic. The first assumption being that diegetic music covers the entire scene, and the second, that incidental music focuses on a specific point.[9]

Diegetic music does not have the dramatic potential of incidental music. If the violent music that Herrmann applied to the shower scene in *Psycho* had come out of a musical apparatus, it would not have had the same effect on the viewer who, because of its realistic nature, would know it could be controlled (the radio could be turned off). Because of that, when one wants to use diegetic music with dramatic effect, certain preparation is necessary. In *The Man who Knew Too Much* (Alfred Hitchcock, 1956), the scene with the most tension takes place during a concert in which an assassin will shoot a foreign prime minister at the moment the cymbals are played. To generate tension and work up to a climax, the director had to make a series of concessions, such as having to explain several times that this was what was going to happen, so that the audience was prepared. There might well be occasions, however, when—without prior preparation—diegetic music is more useful than incidental music for its dramatic effect. An example of this we find in *Rocky* (John G. Avildsen, 1976). In one of the most important scenes, in the central character's seedy bedroom, for the first time he finds the courage to get close to his girlfriend and they begin to show their love by kissing. Instead of incidental music of a typical love song, what we hear is a song they are listening to on the radio. And yet the scene has a tremendous impact. But there are reasons that justify this. The most important is the desire to give the scene and its characters a sober

---

[9] If that orchestra were to play Oriental music, the protagonists, the children, the people passing by and the old people would be listening to and hearing oriental music. The same music, without an orchestra, would have the spectator wondering Who is Chinese here and where is he?

tone. By not having an emotional music accompaniment (incidental music), Rocky and his girlfriend are shown as being simple and humble. If romantic incidental music had been applied, the sequence would be conventional. Furthermore, incidental music is music in movement and, for this reason, in static scenes (a conversation at the table of a restaurant, for example) it is usual to recur to diegetic sources to make the sequence lighter and more agreeable. To put incidental music in a scene of this type, especially if it lasts a long time, could surprise the audience and make them wonder where the music was coming from. The same dialogue transferred to a walk in a park might be accompanied by incidental music without raising an eyebrow.

It is not always necessary that the source of diegetic music be shown in order to consider it as such, but just to make evident that the characters are listening to it or at least that they hear it. In sequences where music is being danced to, even when the source of the music is not seen, it is still considered diegetic. A musical film, however, is an exception to this as it supposes a complete abstraction and does not follow the same rules because of its unique character. With characters singing and dancing without there being any source music, a musical film tolerates and assumes as natural what in other genres would be unacceptable, or at least strange. This is why, in terms of music, musicals form a category of film quite apart.

Diegetic music justifies itself. It is enough that a character put it on or play it for its presence in the scene to be comprehensible. On the contrary, incidental music, which does not have to justify itself to make its presence understood, needs to respond to certain criteria. This is something we will go into later.[10]

Regardless of the differences in their realistic and abstract natures, the spaces they occupy, their duration and all that has been explained earlier, the application of diegesis or incidental music is

---

[10] If a character puts on or plays music in a scene, the spectator cannot question the presence of that music. If a serious mistake is made (as, for example, in a medieval film the characters dance to the sound of 18th century music), the problem lies in the literary script which has so indicated (showing the scriptwriter to not know much) and not in the fact that the character is playing it or putting it on.

extraordinarily useful. With music in diegesis, the characters have control over the music while incidental music, on the contrary, controls the characters. Furthermore, while this is true for the characters, it also works for the spectator. In diegesis, viewers control the music, while with incidental music, they are controlled by it. Imagine what it means to have a character who not only is not controlled by the music, but who directly controls it. First of all, it helps clarify certain aspects about the person him/herself. We can learn a great deal about someone's personality through their musical tastes (*Tell me what music you listen to and I will know what you are like*) In addition, it gives the character greater strength than other characters who are controlled by the music. A few examples:

In *La mariée était en noir* (The Bride Wore Black. François Truffaut, 1967), Jeanne Moreau plays a widow who seduces and then kills all those implicated in the assassination of her husband, which took place on the very day of her wedding. For this, she follows a ritual of playing a record of Vivaldi's *Concerto for Mandolin*. For the audience, the first time she does it is simply an option. The following times she does it, however, it is an act of power. In *One Flew Over the Cuckoo's Nest* (Milos Forman, 1975), with music by Jack Nitzsche, all the incidental music is related to the concept of freedom while the diegetic music used suggests oppression and domination. We have two characters in confrontation—McMurphy (Jack Nicholson, who does not have a single note of music to help him), and the head nurse Ratched (Louise Fletcher), attractive enough but a tyrant. It is she who determines the music the others have to hear and the first battles between the two characters are precisely because of this music. He wants her to turn it off, while she obliges him to listen. A similar thing happens in *American Beauty* (Sam Mendes, 1999), with music by Thomas Newman. Here, the female lead—Annette Bening in the role of an impossible wife—is well reflected in the music she listens to and makes her family listen to while they dine, until her husband blows up and demands, unsuccessfully, that she remove it. But if in these two examples the music put on by a character is evidence of their power, *El laberinto del Fauno* (*Pan's Labyrinth*. Guillermo del Toro, 2006), with music by Javier Navarrete, goes even further. Capitan Vidal, a person absolutely self-sufficient and sure of himself needs no music himself but it is he who has control of the music heard. The pasodobles he plays on his gramophone not only serve to accompany him in intimate moments but the presence of the music—when it filters through to the rooms beside his—ends up representing a serious threat for the rest of the characters. In this film, there is a significant and determining scene for the construction of the music script. Mercedes, who works as servant to Capitan Vidal and who protects the child Ofelia as if she were her own, at one stage sings her a lullaby without words. This lullaby will comfort the little one diegetically in this scene and incidentally in the rest of the film, as it is a theme that the girl inherits and assumes as her own.

In *Up* (Pete Docter, Bob Peterson, 2009), with music by Michael Giacchino, the character—a hero to the protagonist when he was a child—is now a despicable and sinister personage and receives the visit of the other man in his hideout with music that is not exactly welcoming being played on a gramophone. In *District 9* (Neil Blomkamp, 2009), with music by Clifton Shorter, the crazy principal character tries to survive in the ghetto of creatures from outer space in Capetown. However, there are limits that are not in his best interests to go beyond. And these are indicated by the rap music that the dangerous Nigerian drug dealers play on hi-fi equipment.

There are other cases in which the opposite takes place, where characters attempt to take refuge in the music they listen to and who, because they are impeded from doing so by others, grow weaker. In *Vertigo*, Bernard Herrmann centred the music exclusively on that referring to James Stewart and Kim Novak. In the case of Barbara Bel Geddes, where Hitchcock emphasized her forced *chastity* making her out to be a designer of female underwear, Herrmann took absolutely no notice of her, and did not dedicate even one note to her. More complete solitude would have been impossible to show. The only music that is heard is what comes from a record player that James Stewart asks her to turns off as it annoys him. This is an intelligent recourse that functions by contrast. A character deprived of incidental music (while the others are abundantly endowed) becomes a being practically abandoned to her fate. And, in Hitchcock's hands, the result is devastating. In *Rosemary's Baby* (Roman Polanski, 1968), Mia Farrow tries to avoid the stress caused by her neighbours and her problematic pregnancy by listening to jazz, her favourite music. But each time she puts on a record, someone is there to tell her to take it off.

In all these cases mentioned, what was achieved with diegetic music would have been absolutely impossible with incidental music. Music in diegesis—with its many limitations— is a great deal more than simply adding music realistically into a scene.

Incidental and diegetic music are able to coexist in a film, and certainly a musical theme can have both applications within continuity (where we would speak of the transition of diegetic to incidental, or vice versa) or in separate scenes. In *Casablanca*, the song *As Time Goes By* is played on the piano in Rick's Café and later is heard incidentally as a dramatic and romantic reference of the love between the two main characters. But this is not simply a transition of diegetic to incidental music. It is a musical theme that is presented diegetically and, later on, is heard as incidental. In other words, it is a musical theme that is given a double application throughout the film. This ends up being useful to the narration because when the theme is heard incidentally it makes instant reference to that sequence where it was heard diegetically. (This reference takes place in the music script, and not necessarily in the literary script). An example that shows how the opposite can also be done, is seen in *Hush... Hush, Sweet Charlotte* (Robert Aldrich, 1964), where the song of the same name is presented incidentally in the opening credits, to later be applied diegetically coming out of a music-box. Here, the appearance of the music in diegesis does not take the spectator back to the initial reference in the credits, but the opening credits put forward a reference that later will be made concrete (and physical) when the melody appears diegetically. All this, because of the realistic quality of the diegetic music applied.

When diegetic music turns into incidental, we will be faced with a transition that makes possible that it sustain itself in the film and work through the impediments of space and time that are intrinsic to it. As it leaves off being diegetic, a musical theme no longer has a realistic quality and can easily move through other scenes, become more concrete, and have an unlimited duration. But it is obvious that, if the transition of the diegetic to the incidental leaves off being diegetic, then the characters in the film will not be aware of it and only the audience will hear and listen to it. In *Young Frankenstein* (Mel Brooks, 1974), something similar happens to what we talked about in *Hush... Hush, Sweet Charlotte*. The film starts with its opening credits backed by a musical theme by John Morris which, later on, will be interpreted diegetically by characters who play it on the violin. Its importance to the storyline lies in the fact that it is music employed to attract the beast or to calm it. In this sense, its initial application is an early reference. However, there is an even more subtle game at play in this double application. In one specific scene, when Frankenstein's monster has become lost and his owners are trying to find him, they go to the top of a tower and begin to play the melody. In this comic sequence, the monster responds to the call and, attracted by the music, begins to climb the wall tower in an attempt to reach his masters. To emphasize his effort and lighten it with humour giving it a grotesque solemnity, the music immediately begins to become incidental. In fact, the characters on top of the tower have left off playing their instruments to help him up, although the music continues to be heard. When the beast finally gets to the top, the characters return to their instruments and the melody goes from incidental to diegetic again.

The double application makes it possible for the same musical theme to assume all the characteristics of both forms of music, in their corresponding scenes. There are other possibilities that are very useful, as when diegetic music is shifted to other scenes, maintaining the music's point of origin as a reference. That is to say, that parallel actions are opened up and take place while in another scene this same music is heard or played. In *Ragtime* (Milos Forman, 1981), there is an excellent example of this. In the film, with music by Randy Newman, an Afro-American pianist auditions in a club where he wants to find work and plays a ragtime theme on the piano for the owner. The music shifts to other sequences involving other characters in this choral film, to finally go back to the original scene where the pianist ends his audition. The same thing happens in *Catch Me If You Can* (Steven Spielberg, 2002), where a song, *The Look of Love* is heard as incidental music when the protagonist meets a model in a hotel corridor and she offers to spend the night with him in exchange for money. The song serves to resolve another scene in a rather cruel way by means of a parallel montage where we see Carl—the policeman who is tracking the protagonist—in a laundromat, alone and without music, as we then return to the erotic scene. A new cut shows us Carl once more in the laundromat, but now the song is heard here as well, as if making fun of him. As well, in the opening sequences of *King Kong* (Peter Jackson, 2005), a snappy vaudeville song, *I'm Sitting On Top of the World*, is interspersed between the show in the theatre where it is being performed and the street scenes.

In these cases, it is evident that the music has had a double application—diegetic when it is heard by the characters and incidental when it is applied over the whole scene when, even though it is not heard by all the characters, it maintains its diegesis so that those who play or sing it remain present in scenes where they do not appear. It is supposed that what is being evoked is happening in parallel. Why a narrative construction like this is so useful is because the reference to an important scene is not lost, even though it is no longer on the screen and also because it allows different characters to be encompassed by the same music and disposition. In a certain way, what the pianist's music transmits (with a certain melancholic tone, in this case), serves to explain what the rest of the characters are living through, while in the case of *King Kong* it shows the vivid contrast between the happy atmosphere of the theatre with the misery that is being lived in the streets. In *Inception* (Christopher Nolan, 2010), the characters realistically hear the French song *Non, Je Ne Regrette Rien* (sung by Edith Piaf), and this shifts incidentally to the level of dreams, connecting both musical levels in time. The music of the communication with the creatures from outer space in *Close Encounters of the Third Kind* is presented and utilized diegetically until it finally becomes incidental, no longer a vehicle to understand but now a way of engaging the viewers emotionally.

A recourse of this kind allows us to link not only a character with a group of others, but to connect two characters who are not together but can be united through the music, as happens in *Catch Me If You Can.* In a scene in A*tonement* (Joe Wright, 2007) the main character plays a record of the aria *O soave fanciulla, o dolce viso* (from Puccini's *La Bohême*). As he listens to this existing theme, he writes a highly sexual letter to his loved one, whom we see in a different place covered by that same music, used diegetically in his case and incidentally in hers. In this way, the transition from the diegetic to the incidental helps broaden the music's field of action. But it is a transition. When the application changes it leaves off being diegetic and becomes incidental. Can music be both diegetic and incidental at the same time? Only if it becomes a false diegesis, a recourse that surpasses the realism of diegetic music to give it an abstract quality, as in incidental music. It is easily recognized in dance scenes in historical movies when, to emphasize the solemnity, majesty and pomposity of the event, you hear much more (and more intense) music than is objectively called for from the few instruments you see on the screen. We might see a quartet or a quintet of musicians playing music that sounds as if it is coming from at least a dozen instruments. Or a singer accompanied by music played by many more instruments than those we actually see. In this way, the false diegesis permits diegetic music to be used with an incidental disposition. The characters apparently are listening to music that, objectively, it is impossible for them to hear.

In the first sequences of *The Godfather* (Francis Ford Coppola, 1972) there is a false diegesis during the wedding of Connie (Talia Shire). Over the image of the family posing for a photo, we begin to hear a waltz to which Vito Corleone and his daughter dance. The waltz sounds festive, like the other diegetic melodies that are heard in this sequence. However, this waltz does not come from a precise source and, furthermore, a brief crescendo at the end of the scene is heard over the ambient sound. This happens progressively, conferring an incidental rather than diegetic texture to the music, while maintaining the appearance (false) that the characters are listening to music which, in reality, is directed at the film's audience.

In *Elizabeth*, there is a notable false diegesis in the scene where the Queen and her courtiers are waiting on the bank of a river for the boat that is bringing the arrogant French prince. In the boat four musicians are playing to brighten the trip. However, the music sounds as if it were being played by at least twice as many musicians and we even hear instruments that none of them are playing. This is a false diegesis. But there is more. As diegetic music, this ought to sound quite far away when the boat is still at a distance, as we are hearing it along with the Queen in the scene on the bank of the river. Logically, it ought to grow louder as the boat gets closer. But this does not happen. Some time before the arrival of the French prince, the music is already there at the bank of the river, sounding at a completely unreal volume. For this reason there is no logical synchronization in the volume of the music. And that also is false diegesis.

What is the object here? Obviously, to make it seem that the characters are listening to a music that, in fact, would be impossible for them to hear as it is presented in the scene. In the aforementioned *Atonement,* there is a brilliant scene where the realism of diegetic music is violated completely. This is the long sequence that shows the devastating effect of the war, and where a chorus of soldiers sing a song full of hope… and this is heard at the same volume no matter the distance they are from the camera.

In other cases, diegetic music can share its space with incidental music, in a kind of false diegesis, although not exactly that. If, for example, a character is playing a flute (diegesis) and the melody of the instrument is reinforced by an orchestra (incidental), we are not facing a false diegesis, as the character will only be hearing the flute, while the viewer hears all the music. In one case a realistic proposition is served while in the other, it is abstract. This is what happens, for instance, when Jeremy Irons plays the oboe in one of the scenes in *The Mission* (Roland Joffé, 1986), with music by Ennio Morricone that grows beyond the diegesis. However, the false diegesis presumes to make believe that the characters hear the same music as the audience, although that would be absurd. It is, nonetheless, what happens and what is more, quite often in the successful French film *Les Choristes* (The Chorus, Christophe Barratier, 2004) with beautiful music and songs by Bruno Coulais, the songs *Caresse sur l'océan* and *Voir sur ton chemin* are interpreted diegetically by the protagonist choir, they are also heard incidentally and are applied as well as a false diegesis. Furthermore, they are also superimposed simultaneously in both the diegetic and incidental applications, and all with fluidly and great naturalness. The object is evident: to make the spectator participate directly in the musical fiesta taking place on the screen with even more intensity than the very characters who are responsible for the music.

3.3. By what it communicates: necessary and optional

One is not always free to choose the music used in a film. There are times when a film demands a specific music. This music that a precise scene or moment needs is something absolutely necessary and does not apply to *any* music but to that which is specific, clearly defined and recognizable. It therefore does not allow for alternatives. Let us suppose that in a naval scene we see a ship on the horizon. If at that moment we hear *Oh, Britannia*, the spectator will immediately know that the ship is British. Let us imagine another scene in which a couple meets at a party. If in the next scene both are seen walking in Rome and we hear nuptial music by Mendelssohn we would know they have married. Should we be seeing troops marching to the tune of *La Marseillaise* it is not difficult to deduce that the army is French. What happens when we lay in such music? First of all we establish intellectual communication with the spectator who is being given information. It is not so much a matter of provoking emotions as adding knowledge. Secondly, and this is more important, it serves to avoid unnecessary explanations and thus speeds up the rhythm of the narrative or provides an ellipsis. When *Oh, Britannia* is heard this avoids having to show the British flag or the captain calling out something like *Back to London!* With Mendelssohn's march we can avoid sequences from the wedding, etc. As a result, if what interests us is that the spectator knows it is a British ship or that the couple has married, laying in this music makes this immediately evident, moving along the film rhythm and narrative. Thus, necessary music is a tool for establishing intellectual communication. Obviously, it is not any composer's dream to write arrangements for *Oh, Britannia* or Mendelssohn's nuptial march but, if immediate communication is wanted, it must be done.

Optional music is that which *a priori* is not essential to a scene but still may be welcome. This refers to something offered by the composer which helps the film without being an absolute necessity but rather is something quite free and creative. When a composer is asked for a romantic theme, he may write hundreds and while the one selected is considered the best, it would not be the only one that could work. Therefore, what might be considered necessary is the generic character (music of intrigue, of action, romantic music or any other type) as well as that which is not specific. And the communication it establishes with the spectator is emotional.

The examples of necessary music given here have been largely replaced over time. In cinema today we do not see scenes of ships with *Oh, Britannia* as background although this was a frequently-used resource for a long time. Even so, necessary music continues to be much in use in the narrative discourse of film music. It is enough that we want the music to give specific information to the spectator for it to be stipulated necessary to meet this requirement. If we want Spielberg's shark to be present, even if we do not see it, it is more efficient to apply music the spectator identifies with the shark. Not to do so would simply waste time and possibly cause confusion. This means that necessary music has much more importance than music that is not necessary. This is especially so when both are present in the same film which, more often than not, is what happens. This does not imply that optional music is not important; it simply fulfils a role of less narrative significance. The intellectual communication of necessary music implies a need for the audience's understanding and active participation in this communication, whereas the emotional communication of optional music allows the spectator to have a more passive attitude. Both may be compatible and be interrelated, depending on the situation. Optional music may turn out to be necessary when a musical theme that initially had little concrete significance in the development of the music script takes on a specific value and thus is intellectualized. However, this is a process that, if it happens, cannot be turned around. Once an intellectual significance has been attributed to it, its emotional components can be sustained, although its intellectual components will always take first place and any attempt to disconnect them may result in confusion. Its significance may be changed but it will not be without significance.

Later we shall deal with the vital importance of necessary music and talk about the genetic codes or DNA making up this type of music. We shall also amplify matters dealing with optional music, ranging from mere filler music to narrative formulas. While these may not have any genetic content, they can be very useful as secondary themes. Both necessary and optional music serve to communicate with the spectator.

3.4. By attitude: empathetic and non-empathetic

In his book *La musique au Cinéma*, Michel Chion coins a term that, because of its interest, deserves to be analyzed. According to Chion, empathetic music produces an effect that directly follows the sentiment suggested by the scene or the characters—pain, emotion, happiness, etc. Non-empathetic music would be what produces an effect contrary to that suggested by the images. That is to say, pleasant music in tense scenes, agreeable melodies with harsh pictures or just the opposite: very tense and disturbing music laid in over a calm scene. Empathetic music could be considered redundant and, while at times this becomes obvious, at other times it multiplies a specific emotion, which means *more* terror, *more* love, *more* pain. In this way, we synchronize it with what is being expressed in a scene without having to wonder what is going on.

It is not necessary to set out a list of examples of empathetic music because the concept is clear enough and everyone will no doubt remember lots of cases. An example of non-empathetic music is Dimitri Tiomkin's *Strangers on a Train* (Alfred Hitchcock, 1951) in which the crime scene is accompanied by the happy sound of a merry-go-round.[11] Another example is the contrast between classical music and the extremely violent scenes in *A Clockwork Orange* (Stanley Kubrick, 1971), used with powerful effect. Or the editing of parallel sequences which end the first and third episode of *The Godfather,* and also in *The Cotton Club* (Francis Ford Coppola, 1984) where the final killings are respectively choreographed with religious music, an Opera and a tap-dance.[12]

However, non-empathetic music, as such, does not really exist, at least not in any absolute form. The apparent contradiction between

---

[11] In the crime scene there is a notable trick effect with a false diegesis. The assassin and the victim meet for the first time near the merry-go-round and the music sounds at its normal volume. As they leave there in a boat for the island where the murder takes place, obviously the music should also drop in volume. Nevertheless, at the moment when the man strangles the woman, the volume of the merry-go-round music increases and only drops after the crime is committed. This is a way of emphasizing more strongly its non-empathetic nature.

[12] The final sequences of The Godfather and The Godfather, Part III (Francis Ford Coppola, 1990) are apparently similar. In both sequences killings take place while the Corleones go to a event together—a baptism in the first case and an opera performance in Part 3. In both cases there is a religious factor both in the narrative and the music seeing that in the opera a religious scene is being played. In The Godfather, the music is entirely non-empathetic, distant and ceremonial. In The Godfather, Part III, a similar feeling is maintained but here it is combined with the inclusion of one of the main themes of the saga which emphasizes, as opposed to the first Godfather, the unseen presence of Michael Corleone. In this case, the sequence alternates between empathetic and non-empathetic music.

what is being shown on the screen and that heard in the music only emphasizes something that perhaps is not explained in the picture but rather in the music. If the beautiful music applied to a charming landscape is indeed pure empathy, apocalyptic music over the same charming landscape need not necessarily be considered non-empathetic if, for example, it is warning of a coming of catastrophe. Should this be the case, we could then say that there was empathy with what was going to take place. This warning from the music, which would take time to explain in the literary script, would end up becoming clear, or else the spectator would not understand it. In films like *The Godfather* or *A Clockwork Orange*, the aim of apparently contradictory music is to underline the indifference of those ordering or carrying out the violent act, and even to endow it with a ritual character and conveying it in this way to the spectator. In other words, if violence is accompanied by violent music, the spectator will see a violent act. Whereas, if we put non-empathetic music to it, we give the scene a perspective that empathizes with that music.

In the Spanish film *Los Borgia* (*The Borgias*. Antonio Hernández, 2006) with music by Ángel Illarramendi there is a significant sequence where the recently named pope Rodrigo Borgia (now Alexander the Sixth) gathers his sons together to set out the family's immediate plans. At this meeting they decide on acts of vengeance, crimes, settling of accounts and the removal of rivals. The music that accompanies this meeting of these "Corleones of the Renaissance" is, on the contrary, very beautiful and peaceful. It is non-empathetic in terms of the narrative but absolutely empathetic with regard to the point of view of the characters taking part in the scene. They are very happy and this is definitely the perspective given to the spectator. If the director had put music in line with the violence of what was being planned, the reference to the emotions of the characters would have been lost. It was a matter of choosing what role the music should play, for behind a non-empathetic appearance there is always empathy with something although it does not show up clearly in the scene.

What is important is to know what we bring to a scene when we apply music that seems non-empathetic. In *The Village* (M. Night Shyamalan, 2004) there is a fundamental scene where this is done. This is the scene in which we see the invasion of the forest creatures as they come into the village. The terrified people run to hide in the shelters while chaos and fear spread. The protagonist, a blind girl, is frightened and stays in the porch of her house and stretches out a trembling hand in an effort to find out what is happening. What follows is that one of the monsters is observing her. Suddenly, the boy who is secretly in love with her grabs her hand and runs with her to the refuge where they shut themselves in and listen to the terrifying sounds from outside. Just at the moment when the boy takes her hand and up to the end of the scene we hear the splendid sound of the beautiful love theme by James Newton Howard. This melody (which also drowns out a good part of the ambient sound) manages to focus the scene more on the romantic aspect than on the terrifying events. For the director, it was more important to concentrate on this first moment where the protagonists come together, something that will dominate the rest of the film, than to emphasize the terror in a scene where the characters are very frightened. What reaches the spectator is a message of love.

3.5. By allocation: individual, shared and collective

The music may be attributed to a character and thus serve to communicate, emotionally or intellectually, by qualifying, by emphasizing, complementing or making clear aspects of the personage, even when the character does not say a word and it is the music that speaks for him. This then is considered individual music. However, music may be attributed to more than one character—a couple, brothers or a whole family—bringing them under a single concept or emotion expressed in the music. In this way, the group is individualized with respect to the other characters in the film. The music can also be attributed to a much larger group, such as an ethnic grouping, the inhabitants of a country or, slaves, priests, professionals... whatever group that might have something in common. This is shared music. But if there were to be a heterogeneous variety of characters united under the same music, then that music would be collective, uniting what in principle does not appear to be unified. The very story related in the film could be brought under the same musical umbrella with collective music. Nevertheless, this classification of music is not absolute. There may well be music that is neither individual, nor shared nor collective (e.g.

the music used with the shark in *Jaws* or any ambient theme not applied to characters)

If a character has his own music which does not go beyond himself, the music is considered individual. However, should it include another character, it does not necessarily become shared even though it may seem to be so. For example, Nino Rota's love theme in *Romeo and Juliet* (Franco Zeffirelli, 1968) is indeed shared by both characters and belongs to both. Nevertheless, the love theme by Nicola Piovani for *La vita è bella* (*Life is beautiful*. Roberto Benigni, 1998) is music that expresses unilaterally the love of the protagonist for his wife, although later on it ends up being shared.

Individual music assigned to a character may be used in various levels where it can be more or less expressive. When the music gets truly close to the character, explaining or suggesting his thoughts or emotions, unnecessary dialogue can be avoided. Simply by applying the music and making clear its relation to what the character is feeling or thinking will be enough to bring the audience closer to him/her and help them to better understand what is going on. As well as this *interior* music there is an *exterior* music, which does not correspond to the character's emotions or thoughts. It is used wherever the character may be but remains apart from him, either because it belongs to others *(interior* for them and *exterior* for our character), or refers to an ambient context (music of the place where he happens to be) or to some action in which he might be involved, though not emotionally so. Interior music is not necessarily individual as it may be shared. Two people in love walking in a park full of people may share the same intimate and exclusive music that makes their sentiments beautiful and, as it does not refer to an idyllic context, it is not considered collective. With reason, *interior* music has a somewhat more complicated and involved task as it must clarify and explain, whereas *exterior* music can simply provide an ambience. This is one of the great functions of music in film—to get right under the skin of the characters and in some way reveal them to the public. The scope of individual music is very broad in terms of nuances that can be added, but that same amplitude is reduced when the music, either shared or collective, is extended to cover a number of the film's characters. For example, in music shared by two characters (one optimistic and the other pessimistic), any optimistic elements added will inevitably cover the pessimistic character as well, and vice versa. This means that the more characters covered by the music allow fewer nuances as the characteristics must be more general.

Examples of shared music can be found in those contexts where the intention is to give a single voice to a large group of people: the Jewish victims of the Nazis in *Schindler's List*, the Vikings in *How to Train your Dragon* (Dean DeBlois, Chris Sanders, 2010), the adults in *E.T. The Extra-Terrestrial* (Steven Spielberg, 1982), the team lead by Elliot Ness in *The Untouchables* (Brian De Palma, 1987) or, in an even broader sense, the Allied soldiers in *A Bridge Too Far* (Richard Attenborough, 1977), the American soldiers in *Saving Private Ryan* (Steven Spielberg, 1997), the slaves in *Amistad* (Steven Spielberg, 1997), the film crew in *La nuit américaine* (*Day for Night*. François Truffaut, 1973), those that escape in *Argo* (Ben Affleck, 2012). Examples of collective music in the people in *Amarcord* (Federico Fellini, 1974), or in films like *Ragtime*, *A Room with a View* (James Ivory, 1986), *Sense and Sensibility* (Ang Lee, 1995), *Magnolia* (Paul Thomas Anderson, 1999), *Cloud Atlas* (Tom Tykwer, Andy Wachowski, Lana Wachowski, 2012) and a long list of others. In all these cases, the music cannot attempt to be specific but rather, where it is needed, attributes general shared or collective features to the whole group.

Both individual and shared music can be expanded and go beyond either the character involved or the characters sharing it. Expansive music is that which, after starting out being of an *interior* nature moves to become *exterior*, affecting all those around the character responsible for it, or even going much farther. In other words, it is the music of a character alright, but goes beyond his emotions and thoughts to flood over the emotions of others or perhaps the places he moves through. It is very useful and can often make clear the character's enormous power of seduction. However, if it is to work well it must remain clear that it is music belonging to the character (who is *generously* sharing it) and is not the music of the surroundings. One of the best examples of its use is to be found in the marvellous music of Ennio Morricone for *C'era una volta il west* (*Once Upon a Time in the West*, Sergio Leone, 1968). The character of Jill (Claudia Cardinale) has a sweet melody with the soprano voice of Edda Dell'Orso who is seen in an interior shot (revealing her loneliness) but also in an exterior shot where the music expands contagiously, infecting all those around with her infinite goodness. The same thing happens with the character of Guido in *La vita è bella*, where the interior music surpasses his very being and sets out to conquer places and people. There are many other examples where the strength (physical, emotional or spiritual) of a character is defined by music that expands over everything and even silences all other music. Furthermore, while it can spread *goodness*, it can also spread *evil*, as in *The Omen* or in *Atonement*, even if, in the latter case, it is not so much evil as imprudent behavior. Expansive music endows the character to whom it is applied with enormous power, and does it in a way that is quite direct and automatic.

3.6. By connection: integrated and non-integrated

Music can cover a wide range of commitments. The most basic is to serve as a simple aesthetic accompaniment and very often this in itself covers the needs of the film, either resolving them fully or at least in certain sequences. Music can also play a more active role—explaining a scene, a character or the film itself—which it does by absorbing elements of the story or the characters and so becomes interrelated with the image or with some other narrative or dramatic element. This is what can be achieved with integrated music. Its identification with the image or the characters converts it into an indispensable factor for understanding the scene, the characters or the film as a whole. The big difference between non-integrated and integrated music lies in the difficulty, and often the impossibility, of applying the latter in any other film without its losing its meaning and, without this, the scene, character or the film itself is left poorly explained. There are, naturally, degrees of integration, which can all be measured by the damage any part of the film can suffer when deprived of integrated music.

The main theme of *Out of Africa* (Sydney Pollack, 1985), by John Barry, is a beautiful melody which could easily be used in another similar film. And, though it helps the film enormously, the essence of the picture is perfectly explained by the literary script. It is a music that works very well, but which could just as easily function in any other romantic film with a melancholy storyline. On the contrary, John Morris's music for *Young Frankenstein* is integrated. It is justified in the narrative (the characters mention and play it) and it has a direct relation to what is explained. Thus, it would not have the same effect in another film nor would the film for which it was written be properly understood without that music.

The first difference can be found in its creative origins:

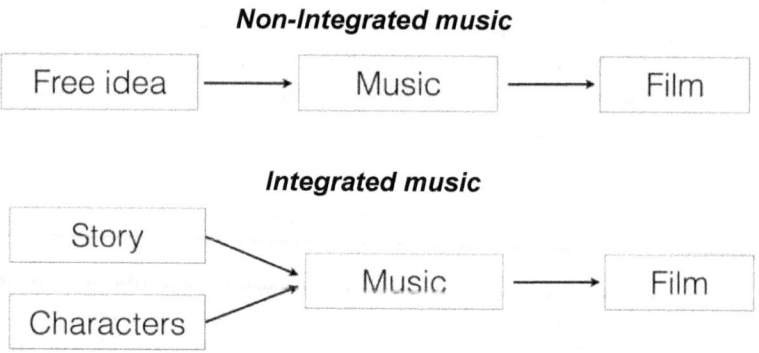

Non-integrated music is the result of general or concrete ideas but always comes out of the personal criteria of the composer or the director. The origin of integrated music comes directly from the image or from the film's literary script. Thus, the composer takes elements of the story or the characters to write the music whose existence is justified by the film script.

The second difference is in reference to the connection:

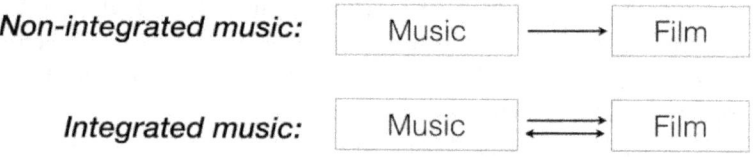

Non-integrated music *feeds* the film unilaterally (music to picture) and, at the highest level, becomes an intrinsic part of it. It complements the film and although it may make it more easily understood, it's not explanatory.[13] On the other hand, integrated music establishes concrete, bilateral connections, so that the music can be understood from the picture and vice versa. If the music is removed from the sequence, this loses a large part of its meaning and ends up being not as well explained. Thus, to add some measure of integration, it is necessary for the composer to transfer to the music concrete elements of the film, and not only aesthetic or emotional elements. If the main character is a violinist and the composer gives a main role to the violin in the music, a degree of integration is established, even if it is minimal. Of course, if the protagonist is Italian and the music is Italian as well, this would also constitute integration. The important thing in any case is that the music work to explain and, in this way, when it is laid in, the film will be more easily understood, not simply more beautiful.

The concept of integrated music should not be confused with that of music that is necessary because they are not the same thing. The difference is in the emotional and intellectual communication that music, which is optional and necessary, establishes with the spectator. Music can be integrated (Mexican music in a film that takes place in Mexico) without it adding any information (and for that reason we could say it was not necessary). However, if the integrated music contains elements that are explicative, it will be or will end up being necessary, and the scene, the character or the film itself will depend on it to be better understood. Naturally, degrees of integration are diverse and must take part in the film in a manner compatible with the non-integrated music used.

This in no way means we should consider non-integrated music as of a lesser category than music that is integrated. The difference between them simply comes down to their greater or lesser implication in the storyline. Duke Ellington's jazz creation for *Anatomy of a Murder* (Otto Preminger, 1959), or that of Miles Davis for *Ascenseur pour l'échafaud* (*Elevator to the Gallows*. Louis Malle, 1957), are extraordinary but could easily be interchanged making little difference to the two pictures. However, another jazz piece, such as

---

[13] The music in a sequence of a car chase, for example, can be written in an intense and powerful manner. It adds dynamism to the action and generates tension. But it does not explain anything other than what the image itself makes clear. It simply reinforces it.

Elmer Bernstein's *The Man with the Golden Arm* is so fully integrated in the film that if the music were removed it would lose meaning and the film would not be as clear. The difference? In the first two examples, the music splendidly sets the ambience, while in *The Man with the Golden Arm* the music explains a great deal about the character that is not dealt with in the literary script.

Some good examples of integrated music:

Sunset Boulevard (Billy Wilder, 1950), with music by Franz Waxman, tells the story of a minor scriptwriter commissioned by an old star of silent movies to write a script for her to make a comeback. The composer took three elements of the script and of the main character. For the first, he used dramatic contemporary music to set the film in the period in which it took place (the Fifties). For the second he wrote a decadent, gothic, sinister and obsessively syncopated tango as a clear expression of the alienation of the character who thought she was living in the golden days of Hollywood (silent films... the age of Rudolph Valentino). For the third, he created a melody vaguely inspired by Richard Strauss' *Salomé*, which was totally justified as this was the character with whom the protagonist dreamed of returning to the cinema. These three elements come together in their most climactic moment in the last sequence when the central character comes down the staircase, facing the cameras and the police, interpreting the great Salomé, the very personage with whom she aspires to make her come-back. In that instant the three elements are magnificently combined—the grotesque situation, the protagonist's paranoia and the absolute decadence of the world that she is abandoning. In this case, the contemporary music applied is not integrated. However, both the tango and the version of *Salomé* respond perfectly to the rules of integrated music—they are justified by the story and make more explicit the madness and decadence of the protagonist. In the same way, without the application of the music, the scene would lose some of its meaning. We could put the contemporary music in another film of the same period, while we certainly could not do this with the tango and *Salomé*.

The Omen is a horror film about a satanic child who destroys everything that resists his power. Its music is by Jerry Goldsmith, whose choral theme *Ave Satani* (and its derivations) is not limited to serve as sequential accompaniment in the film's most terrifying moments, but is a telling expression of the state of mind and the aggressiveness of the child so that, in the face of his lack of expression, the music explains the different degrees of the Devil's anger, to the point where it leads the character.

In *The Elephant Man* there is a sequence where Merrick is humiliated at night by the guard at the hospital, who brings drunks and prostitutes to make fun of him before his old keeper kidnaps him. Apart from a dramatization of The Elephant Man theme, what is heard is the theme played as ballet music. Why ballet music? In the first place, to accompany exactly the tottering as he's being pushed. The music intensifies its strength, then stops when the tottering stops to start up again, after a three-second break, with even greater cruelty. A macabre ballet, it certainly is. But in addition, and much more important, is the fact that Morris twists the soul of the spectator who is made to feel the pain of the humiliation, because he has already been told that Merrick's great dream is to go to the theatre… to see a ballet. And there he has his ballet. This is more effective than incidental music and is, without a doubt, much more painful.

If integrated music is closely linked with the film narrative it becomes necessary and so if we take it away we lose a good part of the sense of the scene where it should be applied. On the other hand, there is nowhere else to put it. There are various degrees of integration that are impossible to classify since it depends on the greater or lesser link they might have with the scene and how much damage might be provoked if the music is removed. The same thing happens when we construct a musical theme for a character. Let us compare two for a single character. In *Pinocchio* (Ben Sharpsteen, Hamilton Luske, 1940), the music by Leigh Harline and Paul J. Smith was very beautiful but at the same time quite basic. It was full of tenderness, innocence and even something of mischief and was certainly not a theme that fell short. It could easily have been applied to any other flesh and blood character but with what was written, it was all that was needed for the spectator to see Pinocchio through the music. Many decades later, *Pinocchio* (Roberto Benigni, 2002) was done with music by Nicola Piovani. In this case, the theme was written with integrated music. The elements making it up were tenderness + mischievousness + clearly Italian music (Pinocchio is Italian) +

wooden instruments (Pinocchio is made of wood) + the important presence of the accordion (his father Gepetto plays that instrument). Putting all these factors together we find the construction of the theme much more closely linked to the character than that written back in 1940, although this was more successful than what Piovani wrote. Both are examples of fine themes although the second showed a more complete degree of integration.

There is another dimension to integrated music which makes it possible to take physical objects from a scene and incorporate them in the music. While they might be invisible to the audience, the music maintains their presence in such a way that anyone watching the film, even though they do not see them, would still be aware of their presence. One objective in this would be to alleviate or lighten up a sequence and make the narrative more fluid without having to see an object which, while essential, is more effectively useful when shown through the music rather than in the visual field. We could say that the soundtrack *steals* the image of the object to return it in the form of music. It cannot be seen but it is there. In this way, we do not need its presence while making it possible to tell other things that the director finds more interesting. To give an example: a clock, which is often used to indicate the passage of time, is fundamental in order to achieve a state of tension. We have often seen shots of the hands or figures of a clock moving inexorably up to an explosion, a crime, etc. What integrated music can do is eliminate the actual presence of a clock while incorporating it in the music so that it is unseen but heard. In this way, the narrative can concentrate on other aspects without having to show the clock. This might be music in which we hear the tick-tock of a clock that is unseen although its presence can be noted. Depending on circumstances, the effect may be much more anxiety-provoking because, through changes in rhythm or cadence, the music may indicate that time is running out. Or the opposite may take place where the music incorporates objects that, *a priori* we do not expect, while their fictitious presence gives greater force to a sequence.

In *Planet of the Apes*, with a soundtrack by Jerry Goldsmith, in the scene of the hunt of humans (when the apes rush in on horseback capturing humans) we hear the sound of hunting-horns, a musical instrument but also a ceremonial one. These are not shown in the visual scene but their music is present. By incorporating these instruments the scene becomes more violent, more grotesque, more terrifying. If the apes were to be carrying those horns and playing them, the effect on the spectator could cause hilarity for being excessive.[14] *The Red Violin* (François Girard, 1999), with music by John Corigliano narrates the odyssey of a violin, passing from hand to hand, from its initial construction by an instrument-maker in the 17th century until it ends up in an auction at the end of the 20th century. The composer, starting out from a main theme defining the instrument, brought in dramatized derivations that, metaphorically, managed to reveal emotions (happiness, nostalgia, depression, etc.) suffered by ... the violin itself! It is not only physical objects that can form part of integrated music, but sounds like the wind, the waves, whistles, onomatopoeias... whatever sound element that brings the music close to the narrative or dramatic aspects of the film.

In *Atonement* Dario Marianelli integrated a typewriter in one of the themes of his score, not for aesthetic purposes but for dramatic and narrative aims. First of all, because the character bringing this music (the girl, Briony) is very much connected to writing and a love of inventing stories. Secondly, and, what is much more important, because of her imagination (in her writing) brings about a tragedy involving her sister and her boy-friend. When this takes place, the theme heard at the beginning of the film resounds now with even greater force, underlining her power over the other characters. And the typewriter reinforces this power. This is so much so that when, later on, Briony now grown up and repentant, we again hear her theme, this time without the sound of the typewriter.

---

[14] Up until this scene, the score has been more suggestive than explicit, given the absence of concrete events. But here the characters are confronted with the first evidence of horror and so, the music immediately makes the chaos evident. A grotesque, wild ballet is evoked, and which seems to choreograph the prosecution. Goldsmith includes those hunting horns, which adds to the confusion and violence. In this way, the audience lives the moment as if they are being hunted. From this moment on, almost everything that is heard is linked to the concept of oppression and violence.

3.7. The impossible timing

Here, I should like to examine a real case and go into detail about how it was resolved. This will be done starting out from a suitable combination of some of the factors analyzed earlier.

Exposition

In the Western *Per qualche dollaro in più* (*For a Few Dollars More*. Sergio Leone, 1965) with music by Ennio Morricone, Gian Maria Volonté plays a bloodthirsty murderer with a macabre fondness for shooting his adversaries just as the music of his watch comes to an end. He challenges his enemies telling them he will shoot when the music stops. The watch's music lasts 60 seconds and, naturally, it is diegetic. There is a very tense scene when the 'bad guy' warns a helpless man that he will kill him *when the music stops*. We know (that is how cinema works) that the man is condemned to die. The murderer takes out his watch. The music begins. However, the agony does not last 60 seconds but goes on past the 90 second mark. When it stops, the murderer fires and the victim is felled. How was this done? Not a single note of music was added to the watch (that would be too obvious) and there was no change of scene.

Solution

The objective here was to increase tension and unsettle the spectator who sees the scene going on and on without knowing how or why. The trick is based on something very simple. Morricone *robs* music from the watch and later on returns it at the end of the sequence. This is the process followed: Volonté opens the watch and the melody begins (diegetic music). Little by little, we begin to hear incidental music in the background and the theme of the watch blends with this melody until it fully integrates with it. Now we are not hearing the watch but the incidental score which incorporates the melody now very much manipulated. As this is unreal music not subject to any determined time it can be lengthened to any degree (within reasonable limits). Finally, it is *returned* to the watch and only this is heard up until it comes to an end. The result is that apparently the music of the watch has not stopped being heard although in reality a melody has been inserted that has distracted the spectator's perception. In order to do this, Morricone carried out a lot of tricks to bring about this confusion. The scene develops in a church converted into a stable and the incidental music of an organ was incorporated in order to give solemnity to the expected death and at the same time prevent the spectator from thinking about the watch. He also used a guitar played in especially low tones in order to draw attention to it and, to make sure that, for a few moments, the viewer would not be thinking about the watch.

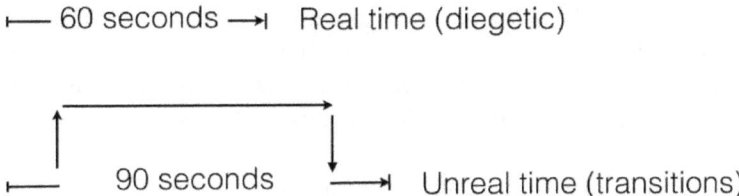

Second exposition

However, this is not all. The scene has been resolved, the trick has been carried out and the spectator's perception has been manipulated. This all works because no one expects that anything like this is happening and there is no time to react. However, if the trick is repeated, there is the risk that, the second time around, the trick could be detected and the effect would be lost. So, here is what happens at the end of the film: the scene with the watch is repeated in real time and immediately afterwards it is repeated again… but this time it lasts for two and a half minutes. The spectator is not aware of the change. How has it been done?

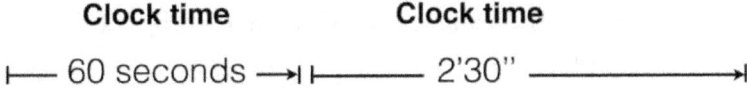

Solution

To begin with, it is quite bold to have the watch sounding in real time and immediately afterwards follow it with the trick of manipulated time. The solution is identical to that set out under exposition: the musical transition diegetic/incidental/diegetic and the integration of the music. However, the viewer would now certainly detect the trick. The key lies in the storyline and particularly in that sequence: in the lack of tension. This is how the scene is developed... the 'bad guy' faces up to one of the protagonists (Lee Van Clift), whose weapon is on the floor. He takes out his watch and warns him that when the music stops he will fire. It will be impossible for the man to retrieve his weapon without being shot at. The scene lasts as long as the watch music sounds. Just as this comes to an end, another protagonist (Clint Eastwood) appears and points his gun at the murderer and then pulls out an identical watch and announces: *You know the game... when the music stops, shoot!* Now the music begins again and the transition already discussed takes place.

In the initial exposition, the music was unidirectional. It came from the murderer and was aimed at the man who was going to die. The spectator knew it would last the length of time the victim had left. This was the kind of agony that, because of its cruelty, would generate enormous tension. This was exactly the same as in the first part of the second Solution. Now, however, things change when Clint Eastwood takes the initiative. Suddenly, the Watch music no longer has a unilateral direction and turns against the murderer. The spectator now knows that its duration will be the same as the lifetime left to the murderer (after all, it is a Western, Eastwood is the hero, it is the final scene and the murderer, the "bad guy", has to die). Suddenly, what earlier brought about tension now generates relief in the spectator. So much so that Morricone was bold enough to include castanets as a mark of celebration at the end of the perverse protagonist. As the scene was such a relief it does not matter that it lasts for an impossible length of time. In fact, the spectator is even thankful for this. When the music goes back to the watch, the murderer drops down dead. This is not just movie music. It is pure cinema.

4. Levels of Music

Within the movie, the music can be placed on different levels where this serves to provide links, to emphasize or add an additional perspective, depending on what is intended. There are four levels of music in film... the perceptive (and sonorous), the narrative, the spatial and dramatic.

4.1. Perceptive and sonorous

A recurring debate about music in film is whether or not it should be heard. Should it be given a prominent place or, on the other hand, is the best music that which is not listened to? There has been a sharp division of opinion on this point, but both views are not only perfectly valid but also compatible. Trying to choose between the concept of music that is listened to and music that is merely heard, the only thought that makes sense at all is that at least the music be heard. Otherwise, why put it in? Music that is listened to is up front and the spectator, aware of its presence, participates more actively in it (becoming more emotional, made to suffer, or whatever). Music that is heard but not listened to functions on a secondary plane and the spectator, not being aware of its presence, remains passive under its influence. This music—heard but not listened to—reaches the spectator through the unconscious. Therefore, it is the level of perception that determines how the music reaches an audience. At the conscious level the spectator can have some control over the emotional impact or the information the music transmits. At the unconscious level, the spectator (not perceiving the emotional impact or the information coming from the music) remains fairly much on the defensive. Both levels of perception, it goes without saying, are especially important in the cinematographic language of music.

Obviously, music that is listened to provokes certain responses in the spectator whereas music that is merely heard brings about a different reaction. The level of perception is not so much a matter of the volume of the music as of the degree of the spectator's awareness.

4. Levels of Music

There is music that is played at a high volume and is not listened to for that very reason. The key is to determine whether or not the spectator is aware that there is music, and the trick is to find just the right balance for it in the film as a whole. Music that is being constantly listened to may become overpowering and not very effective, whereas music that is not listened to when it is needed loses a lot of its meaning, when should the music be put at one level or another? There are many factors to take into account, but the most important is whatever might draw the viewer's attention to what the music has to say (the reason why it should be listened to) or else, what might take the music to the viewer indirectly so that it is not noticeable.

What music from *Psycho* does the audience remember? No doubt, it would be that which was listened to either over the opening credits, the car chase and, of course, over the scene in the shower. In Bernard Herrmann's soundtrack, of course, there is a lot more music than this—in fact, in the 109 minutes of the film, music takes up more than an hour and its effect on the viewer is as, or even more, powerful than usually happens with music that is listened to. Applied at a high level of perception, this music gives the spectator very clear and specific indications—one is afraid of what is going to happen or feels terror because of what is going on. The audience cannot escape because the music is at a close-up level from which there is no way out. On the other hand, music laid in at a low level of perception makes it possible to meet other priorities, such as maintaining the same color or tonality throughout the film, awaiting for the moment when it will be able to have a real effect on the audience, for whom, in any case, it is always present maintaining a continuity of sound. There are other things that music applied at a low level of perception can do as well, such as generate a non-specific tension, provoke a sensation of discomfort or even take the vibrancy out of a scene and make it tedious to watch .And all this without the audience knowing why this should be so, even while the music is giving them information without their being aware of it.

This is exactly what occurs right as the film begins after the opening credits. In the literary script, we see a wide-shot of a city and signs indicating "Phoenix, Arizona, Friday, December 11, 2:43 in the afternoon". The camera makes a tracking shot moving in close to a building toward a window. We go through the window into a room where a couple has just finished having sexual relations and are now getting dressed. Up to this point everything takes a normal course although we see the young woman telling her lover that she is tired of having to give up lunch in order to be intimate with him. In other words, she is not happy and, according to the literary script, the audience has to wait for her to supply this information through the dialogue. However, the musical script has already informed us that she is not happy. Right from the first image following the opening credits and up to when the camera takes us into the room the audience has heard (but not listened to) music so sad and anxiety-provoking that, when the girl speaks, the viewer almost feels sorry for her. This has all been done with subtlety, without any drama, causing a feeling that the audience cannot identify but that inevitably conditions them to consider the girl with a certain compassion.

In *The Sixth Sense* (M. Night Shyamalan, 1999), with a score by James Newton Howard, the greater part of the music runs *underground* almost without being perceived. Its main theme basically serves to generate a constant sensation of loss and sadness that is applied to the main character played by Bruce Willis. Probably, if the music were to be placed at a high level of perception, many viewers would catch on to the film's big secret. This is made clear by the fact that, when this secret is uncovered, the music changes register and now can be clearly listened to. There is another theme that is maintained practically along with the main theme, and it is what accompanies little Cole and his secret, his sixth sense and his fear. The theme evokes the secret he keeps to himself even when he is not present. It only disappears when he loses his fear after helping the phantom girl, thus curing himself and feeling freed. This is achieved at the same perceptive/sound level.

In *Gladiator* (Ridley Scott, 2000), with music by Hans Zimmer, one of the three central themes of the soundtrack (that of the Emperor Commodus) moves always at such a low perception level that it generates a feeling of great discomfort in the viewer. However, the two themes applied to the protagonist (that of the hero and that of the person) which are always evident and clear, the viewer accepts entering into their spirit. Something similar takes place in *The Dark Knight* (Christopher Nolan, 2008) with music by Zimmer and James

Newton Howard. Here, the powerful music that surrounds the figure of Batman is at a high level of perception and this strengthens the character no end while allowing the spectator to be part of it. On the other hand, that applied to the Joker runs at levels that reach the spectator in an unconscious manner. There was a clear attempt to do exactly this. The Joker in this film was not like the amusing or joking character that Jack Nicholson played in *Batman* (Tim Burton, 1989) with music by Danny Elfman. Quite the contrary, he had to be very disagreeable and uncomfortable for the viewer. For that, the face of the actor playing the role (Health Ledger) was made up with battered disfiguring make-up. But obviously this was not enough. A very annoying musical effect was applied over him, a kind of double *glissando,* both simultaneous and alternating, that sounded like the buzzing of a bee. Reaching the ears of spectators unaware of its presence, they naturally attributed the annoying sensation to the character, not to the music. To have put this at a conscious level of perception, we would have been faced with a typical 'bad guy', without any particular effect on the audience's feelings.

The degree of perception the audience has of the music, whether they are hearing and/or also listening to it, is one thing. Something quite different is the volume of the music. Music heard at a high volume does not imply that it is going to be listened to, as it may be sharing space with other sounds and thus become somewhat diluted. On the other hand, music at a low volume may well be listened to by the audience, if it is giving them information they understand. The music often shares its space with other sound—with dialogue, noise, etc. If this is not the case and it stands alone it will be relatively easy to listen to (if this is what is intended). But, should it share space, it will be necessary to find a reasonable balance in the sound so that it can be listened to (again, if this is what is intended). It is quite obvious that against dialogue, the music must find its own volume below it so that the dialogue can be heard. There is nothing worse than not be able to follow the dialogue because the music is too loud (unless, once again, this is precisely what is intended when the director wants to hide the dialogue with the music).

In *Malèna* (Giuseppe Tornatore, 2000) with music by Ennio Morricone, at different moments there are two similar sequences but with a different sound treatment. Each begins with two musical themes—the main theme and a central theme—both used at the beginning of the film. In the first of these similar sequences we see the attractive protagonist, dressed provocatively walking across the town square under the lascivious glances of the men and the envious looks of the women. Malèna walks around the square and sits at an outdoor café, takes out a cigarette and several men rush to offer her a light. The sequence is accompanied by the central theme followed by the film's main theme, one after the other. The central theme is a popular Italian melody, jovial and carefree, which reflects the feeling of the town. The main theme is that of Malèna—warm, tender music that is beautiful but not without some sadness. Both themes come in at a high sound level.

Music: ——Central theme —— I —— Main theme ——
Sequence: ....

In this way, the music carries out its first task of setting the scene (the square filled with people) and then its dramatic task (with the start of the Malèna theme, the music supports her rather than the surrounding situation), still giving absolute equality to both themes. It highlights the protagonist and follows her during her walk around the square. Later on, in the final moments of the film there is a similar sequence. The square is again full of people and Malèna crosses it. The narrative circumstances, however, have changed.[15] The same central theme is repeated followed by the main theme but this time the sound levels are different.

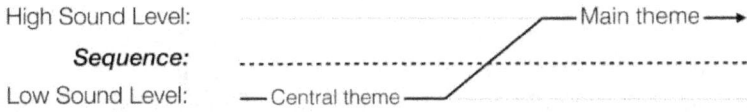

When the central theme is at a low sound level, what we hear up front is the sound of the town square ambience (noise, voices,

---

[15] Here is a synopsis: in a Sicilian town during WW II, a beautiful woman whose husband is off at the war is trying to survive poverty. Believing her husband is dead, she ends up as a prostitute for the Germans and when the war ends she is expelled from the town. The sequence shows her return on the arm of her husband.

shouts, etc.). When the change is made to the main theme, which plays at a high level, the ambient sound drops so that the levels of the music and the ambient sound are interchanged.

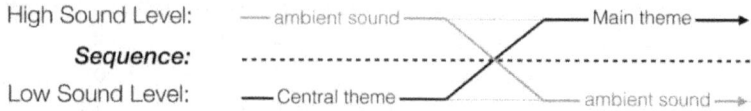

In the previous sequence, the ambient sound and the sound level of the two themes were in the same range. Now this is not the case and a different effect is produced. In both the previous scene as in this one, as well as in relation to the central theme, preference is given to the main theme. In this way, and this is important, whereas before the music was limited to highlighting Malèna, it now serves to isolates her from her surroundings. In something like a close-up carried out by the music, we get the impression that there is no one else but her in the square. In fact, and this is also important, the Malèna theme starts before the camera shows her. Initially, it is heard over the surprised looks of the townspeople and we realize, through the music, that Malèna is there even though she is not yet seen. And when she does appear it is in a wide-shot in the distance. But the (musical) close-up of her has already taken place. Later, successive shots will certainly come close to her face, but the music which came before this visual effect will have isolated her from the general surroundings. To do this it was fundamental that the two levels of music take part in the scene.

Making the ambient sound disappear in order to leave the music at a single sound level serves to automatically underline the importance of this music, as well as being a narrative and emotional resource that works well. It forms part of the tricks that can be used with the levels of perception and sound. The music takes up all the sound space in the kiss sequence with the circular tracking shot in *Vertigo*, as with the appearance of the *Adagio for Strings* in *The Elephant Man*, already commented upon. The same thing happens when E.T. *The Extra-Terrestrial* begins to fly, and also in *Up*, and in *How to Train Your Dragon*. In these cases, if we take out the background noise and sounds, which logically should be present in the scene, what the scene's musical theme transmits is magnified and reaches the spectator in the form of a "close-up". A notable and daring example is what takes place in *Munich* (Steven Spielberg, 2005), specifically in the editing of sequences where we see the protagonist having sexual relations with his wife, while the tragic events that happened in the Munich airport, with the terrible massacre of those kidnapped and of the terrorists--both sequences fused together by the main theme by John Williams, the beautiful and tragic lament in the voice of Lisbeth Scott, which fills the entire soundtrack until it silences the shots, the explosions and screams, but as well completely silences the sounds which should be heard in the room with the protagonist and his wife.[16]

4.2. Narrative

The film *La nuit américaine* has two narrative levels. At one level, there is the shooting of a film while, on the other, the film being shot. Georges Delerue, the composer, wrote the music for both so that the essential level of the film (the shoot) has its own music while the fictitious level (the film the characters act out) has its own. Delerue puts his score on two different narrative levels, underlining them both. The film *Altered States* (Ken Russell, 1980), in turn, narrates the experiences of a doctor who goes beyond the frontier of reason when he tries out experiments on himself, which take him into an unreal world. The real-life sequences were handled differently from the dream sequences by composer John Corigliano who put his score at two different narrative levels. A film can have either a single narrative level or several (combining the present with the past, the real with the dream world…) A composer may also choose to mark or not the differences between these levels or, when there are no distinct levels, pace the events that take place, as happens with the music by Victor Young for *Around the World in 80 Days* (Michael Anderson, 1956). Young's score is adapted to the geographical and narrative situation (Spanish music in Spain, French music in France…), or is completely

---

[16] In the part corresponding to the violent massacre at the airport, Spielberg occasionally lets us hear some bursts of machine-gun fire (but only a few). What might seem merely an aesthetic option has, in reality, a powerful dramatic effect. In a way, the director is reminding the viewer that violence has its own sound, but by then silencing it with Williams' music, underlines that what this music expresses is much more important.

synchronized with the period in which the story takes place. This is what John Addison did with his amusing Baroque music for *Tom Jones* (Tony Richardson, 1963).

If a film takes place in a specific location or is set entirely in a determined historical period, it would make sense that the music reflect that place or period. Should this be the case, it would match what the film deals with at the narrative level. This happens in *Havana* (Sydney Pollack, 1990) where there was substantial use of Caribbean music written by Dave Grusin; in *Frida* (Julie Taymor, 2002), a film biography of the painter Frida Kahlo with Mexican music by Elliot Goldenthal; and in *Gandhi* (Richard Attenborough, 1982) where all the sequences dealing with local people had Indian music by Ravi Shankar, while those relating to the British were accompanied by music of the British composer George Fenton. If a film takes place in a military context, it is obvious that the music would have a martial tone: Max Steiner's music for *The Caine Mutiny* (Edward Dmytryck, 1954), or Elmer Bernstein's score in *The Great Escape* (John Sturges, 1963).

But does this always have to be the case… if a film set in Mexico or one taking place in the Middle Ages, what point would there be not to use Mexican or mediaeval music? The main reason not to respect the film narrative would be to find a universal significance in what the film is all about. In other words, allowing the music (neither Mexican nor mediaeval) to convert the location into something purely circumstantial, making more relevant what is being related rather than where or in what period it takes place. If we lay mediaeval music in a film based on Shakespeare's Hamlet, the spectator will expect a mediaeval story. If we put music from the 20th century, it will be a universal and timeless story, not simply one from a specific period.

In *The Hours (*Stephen Daldry, 2002), by Philip Glass, there is no distinction in the music treatment given to what takes place in the Twenties, in the Fifties, or at the beginning of the 21st century. The fact that the music is not synchronized with the literary script at the narrative level, helps to give a timelessness to the stories. Of course, it may happen that the music does try to respect the film's narrative line but through a false approach. The music by Miklós Rózsa for *Ben-

Hur (William Wyler, 1959) is intended to sound Roman when clearly it is not; and Nino Rota's score for *Romeo and Juliet* is contemporary romantic, despite the notable presence of mediaeval instruments. If there is something 'false' in the narrative level of the music, it may well have been intended. What music could there have been in *Journey to the Center of the Earth* (Henry Levin, 1959) if it were not music invented at the narrative level?

4.3. Spatial

In a film sequence, the music may be located in different spaces, thus affecting not only how the audience sees it but determining the perspective. This all depends on the action, the emotions, the references and the music brought forward.

1.– Spatial level of action

Imagine a film sequence in which a girl is running through a forest with the camera following her. In visual terms and in the literary script what we see is a girl running through a forest. If over this we put music for running that is what the audience will see: a girl running. Is she late for an appointment? Is she looking for someone? We cannot tell. She is simply running and the music only tells us that she is running. This music stands at the spatial level of the action.

2.– Spatial level of the emotions

In the same sequence we can decide not to put music for running but music of fear. In this case, what we see is a girl running with a feeling of fear. The information we have is much greater than in the previous case. There is some reason for her need to run: is she running away from something? Must she hurry before something terrible happens? This music stands at the spatial level of the emotions. Now, to whom does this emotion belong?

2.1.– Spatial level of the character's emotions

It is the girl who is afraid. And this is why she is running. Now the spectator knows that she is afraid and why she is running. If this does not affect the audience (let us suppose they want her to suffer) then the audience is not involved in the sensation of panic and the music stands at the spatial level of the character's emotions.

2.2.– Spatial level of the spectator's emotions

The girl is running but she is not feeling afraid. It is the audience that is feeling this. She perhaps thinks she should hurry to find her lover who is about to go away. But she does not know (while the audience does) that someone is following her with the intention of killing her. The girl lacks the information that the audience knows and at the spatial levels the music stands with the audience's emotions and not those of the character.

2.3.– Spatial level of the emotions of the character and the audience

The girl is running very scared (she knows they are following her) and the audience is suffering along with her. Both of them (the character and the audience) share this fear and thus the music settles at the spatial level of the emotions of the character and the audience.

In the above three suppositions, we have not changed a single frame but following the three options we see three quite different sequences. While this may be obvious, it should be noted that the spatial level of the action in each case and that of the emotions may be compatible. That is to say, it is possible to use *music for running because of fear* even though the spatial level of the emotions is always above that of the action and the audience will be more aware of it. If we opt for placing the music only at the spatial level of the emotions what is important is to delimit whichever one of the three is chosen.

The key in this case is knowing how to apply the music at any one of the three spatial levels of emotion so that the audience can understand the direction being taken. What is very important is the planning of the scene and, even more, the information the audience has and how much they are involved. As already mentioned, it may be that they feel little concern about the suffering of the character. If this is the case, it may well be that the music speaks only of the character's emotions and that the audience feels quite indifferent. Or it sometimes is intended that these emotions be shared between character and audience. For example, when the protagonist of *Lawrence of Arabia* (David Lean, 1962) is travelling across the desert by camel, the beautiful music by Maurice Jarre is expressing not only what this man is feeling but wanting to call on the audiences' emotions at the grandeur of the desert landscape. It is, therefore, music at the spatial level of the emotions shared by both character and audience.

If we wish to distance the spectator from the emotion of the character, it is necessary that there be something in the literary script to make this separation clear. Music alone cannot do this. By the same token if, thanks to the literary script, the audience is aware that a character does not feel the emotion transmitted by the music, this will settle at the spatial level of the audience's emotions, but not of the character. This supposes there must be an interrelation between what is explained in the literary script and what is indicated by the music script. Because, as we continue to stress, music can help clarify or explain many things but it does have its limits.

Let us take an example. A police officer has infiltrated a mafia organization in order to help dismantle it. In a particular scene, he manages to get one of the mob to present him to the most powerful (and dangerous) bosses of the clan. Now, the police officer is surrounded by the most fearsome types in the city. Here we have danger at its highest level. Does this call for high-tension music? That would certainly be the most suitable for the situation. But, what if we want to avoid giving the impression that the character feels any fear... that not only does he not feel afraid but is in fact completely calm? If we do not put music because the character is calm, we remove tension from the sequence and the emotion will not reach the audience. How can we fill the sequence with tension without implicating the character who is most at risk? This is what happens in *Donnie Brasco* (Mike Newell, 1997) with music by Patrick Doyle. Johnny Depp arrives led in by a somewhat imprudent Al Pacino. He is right here in the middle of the most powerful mafia chiefs and during the scene we can feel enormous tension through the music (which is not great music nor did it have to be but indeed it is very useful). How does Johnny Depp keep out of all this? Quite simply, just by taking him out of the scene and always keeping him on a second plane or even somewhat out of focus. Anything to not involve him in what the music is getting across to the audience. If, on the other hand, Johnny Depp were in close-up and always well in focus, he would inevitably be seen as being implicated in the music and would give the sensation of being tense. The more a character is maintained marginalized from the music, the closer he will be to the audience if they feel empathy for him. However, as we already saw in the great final sequence of *Per qualche dollaro in più,* there would be no problem where the audience remains indifferent to the suffering of the character for whom it has no empathy.

3.– Spatial level of references

Let us go back to the girl who is running in the forest and let us suppose that she is running with the accompaniment of music we know, that of her boy-friend, for example. If the spectator understands that this is her boy-friend's music, the music will be referring to a person who is not on the screen nor is being cited in the literary script. At the spatial level of references, the music adds an element, a character or an object previously identified in musical terms, which the spectator already knows. Therefore, by its being applied at this spatial level we would understand the girl is running because she wants to be with her boy-friend.

The spatial level of references obviously demands that the identification brought by the music applied be heard and understood by the spectator. If this is not so, it will not have any narrative effect at all. Its special usefulness is that it avoids having to cite or mention what is referred to in the literary script as this has already been done by the music script. This spatial level facilitates intellectual communication with the spectator as it serves to put something into the scene that does not have to be mentioned in the literary script. In various scenes, in any part of the trilogy *The Lord of the Rings* (Peter Jackson, 2001-2003), for example, the ring is put right there by the music that Howard Shore used to refer to it, without the characters having to mention it.

4.– Spatial level of brought forward music

Up until now, of the various options of spatial levels considered, we have looked at the possibility of putting music that fits what is happening in the scene, whether in the action, in the emotions or in references made. However, what if the music is not related to the scene in any of the senses mentioned? In other words, can music be inserted in a sequence to which it does not correspond either in narrative or dramatic terms? In the first scene, that of the title credits of *The Silence of the Lambs* (Jonathan Demme, 1991), with music by Howard Shore, we see Jodie Foster doing physical exercise in a forest, running and jumping over obstacles. It is a daily routine (a girl exercising) which, however, is accompanied by music somewhat apocalyptical and decidedly intriguing. However, nothing in the action makes us think that something terrible is going to happen to the girl while she is exercising. Nor does this come out in the actions or emotions of the character. Neither does it serve as a reference. Then what purpose does it serve? The answer to this brings up one of the most important keys to the use of music in film—the bringing forward of events still to come. The music does not express anything about what is happening right then but sacrifices narrative synchronization to suggest something that is to take place later on. To some extent, we know that nothing is going to happen to the girl while she is doing her exercises but through the music we imagine that later on something bad is going to happen to her. This is a stratagem very much used and one of which Bernard Herrmann was a master, to the point where we could call it the much imitated *Herrmann method:* the use of music before the events take place where it will finally apply. The British film The *End of the Affair* (Neil Jordan, 1999), set at the time of the Second World War, tells how a woman begins an ardent romance with a writer which she breaks off to keep a sacred promise made to save his life following a bombing raid. Long before the drama comes to a head and while the lovers enjoy their passionate relationship, the composer Michael Nyman gives advance notice of what is going to happen to them through music of romantic feeling with a somewhat contained tone of tragedy, suggesting a state of latent desolation. This serves to give the audience early warning that they are watching a drama which will end badly.

4. Levels of Music

There exists a golden rule with regard to the specific placing of the music in relation to the development of the narration. It may be heard parallel to the events in the film or it may come beforehand but never afterwards. In other words, the music cannot come in late for its application in the film. If it does so, it serves no purpose. An action may be accompanied by the music (parallel). It also may anticipate events that have not yet taken place (prior) where it warns of something about to occur before it happens. This is exactly what we see in the scene of the nighttime car race in *Psycho*, a notable sequence because it tries to confuse the spectator. At first, everything suggests that the music is being heard at the spatial level of the action and the emotions (it describes a specific action in which the girl is anxiously driving a car). However, at a determined moment the protagonist smiles. Despite the fact she smiles and seems more relaxed (in reality she is feeling triumphant), the music does not change. Therefore, the music does not remain at the same spatial level of the emotions (of the character), although it stays at the spatial level of the action. However, as the girl is now driving her car quite calmly, but the music is no longer at the spatial level of the spectator's emotions, the scene as a result loses some of its tension. But the music continues on in the same vein without let-up. In fact, the music is driving the protagonist (and the spectator) to a specific place, namely the motel where she is to be killed.[17] The music remained at the spatial level of the brought forward music.

Of course, the music cannot be placed after the events that it is attempting to underline. In *Jaws* there is a sequence where the three men who are trying to find the shark throw meat into the sea in order to attract it. Suddenly, and without any warning from the music, the huge creature appears, scaring both the protagonists and the spectators. Immediately after--but after—the music returns. The effect is powerful because it catches the spectator unaware. Williams explained it this way: *"we know now the shark really is there, but we haven't advertised it with music, so its attack comes out of silence. Now, because you would have been conditioned to hear music every time and we don't, when the shark arrives is more terrifying"*.[18] Here,

---

[17] In fact, the last notes of Herrmann's music coincide with a shot of the ill-fated motel. Herrmann explains the message: "Something terrible is going to take place and it will happen right here."

the music comes in immediately after the visual impact of the shark's appearance but within its trail so that, with only a second's delay, it becomes a parallel action. If, on the contrary, it had been delayed five seconds it would not have any effect on the spectator. It would have come too late. The fact is that the music is of little use if it tries to provide information that the viewer already knows through the course of the film. If, for example, the composer tries to hide the fact that a character is a murderer when the spectator already knows he is, even though he has not yet killed anyone, any music used to hide this would be of no value. And even less so, if the music laid in has already made evident that he was a killer. It would add nothing and would be purely superfluous information.

4.4. Dramatic

Dramatic levels establish the different emotions on which a film is structured musically. Normally, there are various dramatic levels adding their specific color: romantic, dramatic, horrific, hateful, etc. However, within each of these colors it is necessary to decide on the tone. What kind of romanticism? Is it happy and jovial romanticism? Is it melancholic, fatalistic or pessimistic? The better we determine the exact color of each dramatic level, the clearer these will be for the spectator. Keeping in mind that a musical theme can change its own color (a happy romantic theme can become sad, for example), level (music for love can become the music for hate), or within one dramatic level there may be various musical themes, some of them changing while others remain static. From this we may deduce how important it is to have a well-defined dramatic level for the film. In fact, the spatial levels only determine whether we place the music as reference in the sphere of the action or in the emotions (of the audience, the character or of both). However, this only determines the placing and not the emotion it transmits. Because of this, by precisely establishing the dramatic level of the music placed, for instance, at the spatial level of the character, makes what is being felt totally understandable.

---

[18] Composer's comments on the making of the movie, included in the DVD edition of the film.

4. Levels of Music

The dramatic level refers to emotions. A music used for the Montagues and another quite different for the Capulets in *Romeo and Juliet* does not mean a double dramatic level but rather a narrative one. Only if one should be accompanied by music expressing hate while the other is given music of love, would this be a double dramatic level. And if there exists the dramatic level of love, we could accept all the possible manifestations of love (all the variants in their own colors) within it. In the French film *Le fabuleux destin d'Amélie Poulain* (Amélie, Jean Pierre Jeunet, 2001) the music by Yann Tiersen has the unmistakable flavor of Paris (narrative level) but goes through various dramatic levels—the joy of life, love, melancholy, innocence and also goodness, among others. In *The Adventures of Robin Hood* (Michael Curtiz, William Keighley, 1938), one of the great classics of adventure movies showing the struggle of the Sherwood forest hero against a corrupt king, the music by Erich Wolfgang Korngold gave the underprivileged (specifically the hero) a majestic and brave treatment which raised him to the category of a real king, a defender of the poor and of noble causes. The vitality and optimism of this music stood against the arrogance and pomposity expressed musically for the powerful. In *The Passion of the Christ* (Mel Gibson, 2004) the images are of extreme violence but the music by John Debney incorporates a dramatic level that is spiritual, mystical, very beautiful and not at all violent. There is no Garden of Eden in *Il buono, il brutto, il cattivo* (*The Good, the Bad, the Ugly*. Sergio Leone, 1968), but it is there thanks to Ennio Morricone's music, especially in the scene where *the Ugly* reaches the cemetery and begins his frantic and desperate search for the tomb with the inscription that will take him to a substantial treasure. In this sequence, the music is euphoric, ever increasing in intensity and aided by the soprano voice of Edda Dell'Orso. Morricone does not focus on the character's avarice but provides a more mystical, even biblical, concept: the arrival at the *Promised Land*. Thus, the music is tremendous as well as very bright and happy.[19]

---

[19] Morricone made a number of Westerns but it was those of Leone that would bring him fame. Faced with the epic dimensions of the Americans Moross and Bernstein, he opted for not repeating that formula, which was certainly successful, choosing to work with more mystical criteria which better suited Leone's films. While in the United States, preference was being given to the territorial aspect of the music (that is to say, the spot where the film takes place), his idea was to provide a sense of time so

4. Levels of Music

The erotic dreams of the protagonist in *American Beauty* take up a small segment of the film but the music by Thomas Newman deals, to a large extent, with those dreams. There is no realistic intent to refer to a description of characters or situations, but rather to play up the dreamlike quality and increase the sense of confusion and vague obsessions, giving priority to the state of latent chaos which makes it possible for the character's sexual fantasies to appear natural, and thus acceptable, to the audience. The composer deliberately uses an undefined and ambiguous style of music which is very practical in the film. In these cases, the music incorporates a new perspective which ends up being explanatory: the transformation of certain arid celestial landscapes or the constant presence of a lascivious obsession. The terrain in which things move when a dramatic level is applied is much wider and freer and the options are infinite because, while the spatial level (that of the emotions, for example) determines only the perspective (that of the audience, of the character or of them both), the dramatic level emphasizes the explanation for those emotions.

If the music goes deeply into the emotions of a character and makes very clear what kind of emotion is being felt (especially when the character seems to want to hide or explain it), it contributes to our defining that character, who without the music would remain incomplete. The thriller *Double Indemnity* (Billy Wilder, 1944) saw the start of the fruitful connection of Miklós Rózsa to *cinema noir*. In

---

that the music would serve to set the film within Humanity's most primal epochs and thus give it the biblical sense that the director was looking for: in characters that come from nowhere, in towns without a past, and a social environment that looked as if it had been only recently formed. It became like an emulation of phrases from Genesis: "In the beginning God created the Heavens and the Earth; the Earth was chaos and confusion. And then he created Man. Within this concept he developed a formula that he would apply in the credits of several of his films, which consisted of a simile of Creation: it began with rough and primitive sounds (the music of the primitive Earth), then went on to incorporate percussion and other more conventional instruments (the origin of Life) and ended up using human voice and orchestration (the appearance of Man). This was when the stories began. Because of this, it was logical to use instruments that were the least conventional possible and, at the same time, employ primordial sounds: whips, blows on an anvil, the lowest registers of a guitar, bells, howls, screams, a harmonica...anything that might evoke an idea of "the origin of Man" and especially those that might give a sense of violence. He contrasted all this with the voice of his inseparable soprano Edda Dell'Orso and the overall result was perfect.

this film, Rózsa emphasized the most obscure and perverse aspects of the relationship between Barbara Stanwyck and Fred MacMurray, as well as of her enigmatic and absorbing personality, avoiding any romantic aspect, emphasizing instead the carnal desire and the brutality of them both when they decide to kill her husband. Something quite different happened in *Spellbound* (Alfred Hitchcock, 1945), a film that, for the period when it was made, could not be explicit about what was obvious in the story—the sexual attraction of Ingrid Bergman for Gregory Peck. As the literary script could not explain this, it was done through Rózsa's music. For example, in the sequence at night where, unable to sleep, she ends up going into his room accompanied by a passionate melody which, under its romantic tone, underlined a strong impression of desire.

At the dramatic level, music can become involved in the characters' desires, making them obvious when they do not yet exist in the film. In *Who's Afraid of Virginia Woolf?* (Mike Nichols, 1966), composer Alex North underlined the protagonists' bitterness, leaving all the weight of fury and anger to the dialogue. As a result, against the desperate battle that the couple engage in right throughout the film, his beautiful music remained in clear contrast to the battle carried out on the screen. The nature of the characters often determines the dramatic level of the music accompanying them although at times a director may opt for counterpoint, as in *The Adventures of Robin Hood*. However, if the characters are simple and not very sophisticated, it is logical that the music, too, be simple and unsophisticated in line with the characters to make them better understood. It is enough to recall the score by Georges Delerue for the film *La peau douce* (*The Soft Skin*. François Truffaut, 1964) or that by Luis Bacalov for *Il postino* (*The Postman*. Michael Radford, 1995) among many others that clearly line up the music with the characters. This "levelling" has not always been fully understood, as happened with the soundtrack of *Rocky* which was accused of being vulgar and sounding like discothèque music. Nevertheless, it is a sample of the good use of music at the dramatic level. In this magnificent film there is scarcely any music except near the end. The semi-documentary tone of the film and the intrinsic nature of the characters (simple people, anti-heroes) would have lost some of its efficacy if composer Bill Conti had put conventional music to the film. Except at the very end, there are scarcely any melodic suggestions during the film, something deliberately kept to a minimum. On the other hand, in the scenes prior to the final fight, the powerful song *Gonna Fly Now* gave Rocky his only heroic moment, the only time he was given any emotional backing. Even though he does not win the fight and his character remains still a poor loser, the music finally provided him with the warmth he had been lacking all through the film. The vulgarity of the discothèque theme was questioned without considering that this was the type of music a character like Rocky would have listened to in real life... Rocky would never have listened to Mahler!

In any case, if the music can be applied in favour of a character, it may also be made to work against him or her. Let us go back to the *musical chase* worked out by Elmer Bernstein for the character played by Frank Sinatra in *The Man with the Golden Arm,* or the announced fatality in scores such as that of Max Steiner in *The Treasure of the Sierra Madre* (John Huston, 1948), Howard Shore's music for *Se7en* (David Fincher, 1995), or what happens in the film *Los abrazos rotos* (*Broken Embraces*. Pedro Almodóvar, 2009) where composer Alberto Iglesias is the enemy in the relationship between Penélope Cruz and Lluís Homar. The music does not side empathetically with the characters but always hampers their way toward redemption or happiness and even punishes them. Their intimate meetings end up being less and less amorous or sexual. The music hangs over them like a threat of disaster, which converts those scenes into moments far from happy. It is highly significant that the only time when the two are able to free themselves from this harassment (in the scenes where they travel to Lanzarote in order to be away from her obsessive husband), Iglesias' music does not come into the picture and a song is dropped in right at that point. Once the composer's music reappears things again start to go wrong. In this film, they were working on two clearly defined dramatic levels. On the one hand, there was music for suspense and mystery and, on the other, music dedicated to emotions. The suspense themes cause uncertainty, are applied indiscriminately and involve and affect many of the characters. But they are mainly aimed at the spectator. The music dealing with the emotions, as already pointed out, has the objective of hanging like a threat over those who want to be happy. It is almost unbearably dramatic and is applied at a spatial level of the characters' emotions (not those of the audience).

Spartacus (Stanley Kubrick, 1960), with music by Alex North, has two quite different dramatic levels. One is the hostile environment, maintained from the beginning to the end, reflected by music which appears to be chaotic, violent, harsh and martial, symbolizing both Roman oppression and Spartacus's struggle. In this very arid landscape paced by the music a theme of love is heard—a sweet simple melody based on just three notes that stand out like a flower in a vast desert. The contrast has tremendous impact. It reinforces the very essence of the romantic theme and defines the two protagonists (Spartacus and his beloved) by its absolute simplicity. The music in *Jaws*, on the other hand, has a very intelligent double level, neither of which is narrative but dramatic. There is the level linked to the sea bottom and another outside the water. Then there is the music for the shark and its environment, and that for the humans. These are two antagonistic positions where the more sophisticated, most elaborate music is that coming from the sea, where the seriousness of the underwater music is in contrast to the light and deliberately banal melodies John Williams wrote for the exteriors: a clear emulation of the enormous power and wisdom of the shark as against the dull, lack-lustre heroism of the humans. To emphasize these differences, he used a trivial Baroque divertimento heard as the tourists arrive *en masse* in the town.[20], along with a pastiche of *korngolian* fanfare which, while appearing to underline the fishermens' skill, makes evident their incompetence. In *One Flew Over the Cuckoo's Nest* there is a double dramatic level in Jack Nitzsche's music, which is established in function of its incidental or diegetic application. All of the incidental score is linked to the concept of freedom (which is what the protagonist is seeking), while the diegetic music expresses the concept of oppression. This is the music that the unsympathetic nurse Ratched obliges her patients to listen to and which Jack Nicholson rebels against demanding her to turn it off.

---

[20] This theme which on the CD of the soundtrack Williams ironically titled 'Tourists on the Menu'.

5. Distribution of Music

There are three ways of handling music for a film. In two of them, the film as a whole is taken into account and an attempt is made to give it some kind of coherence, not necessarily with stylistic unity but at least with a certain color or intent. Later, it can become more detailed while keeping in mind what has already been done or what is to be done in the rest of the film. These are soundtracks with a themed structure or without. In the third method, the director works without this criteria and the music is laid in at different parts of the film independently of what may have been done or what is going to be done in other sequences.

The latter method of applying music is often (though not necessarily) due to a lack of criteria, not knowing what to do or perhaps even to a lack of interest. When this is the case, the music turns out to be a patchwork that, while it more or less serves specific needs, does not help to strength the film as a whole, either aesthetically, emotionally or in its narrative. At times, this may be due to the ineptness or inexperience of whoever has taken this decision. However, it can also be part of a calculated plan and produce brilliant results. We see this in some of the films by Quentin Tarantino such as *Pulp Fiction* (1994), in which the heterogeneity of existing music is applied in order to resolve scenes but without an overall unity in mind. There are several reasons for this. It may be to break the film down into independent sections, to generate a sensation of chaos and disorder or, in general terms, simply not to delegate narrative or emotional aspects to the music. These may function as sharp turn-arounds, but most films that work like this lose a good opportunity to make better use of the music and the results are generally mediocre.

On the other hand, in the first two methods there is an overall view and some kind of interrelation between the musical themes. Before beginning to write the composer needs to answer questions such as: what kind of music does the film need? What emotions must be given priority in being aroused? How is the music going to be distributed? How much music? How many themes and, where there is a themed structure, which will be central or secondary themes and which characters will require them? How should the music begin and how should it end? The composer needs a strategy in which, first of all, he deals with the film as a whole and then with concrete and specific aspects such as the various sequences. In this way, one can plan not only how to make the film more complete but also how to endow it with a certain logic.

What marks the difference between these two ways of working is the presence or absence of a themed structure. A composer who uses the same theme in more than one sequence is already, in reality, interlacing various parts of the film and therefore establishing a connection throughout the footage, even if it should be only of a basic and elementary nature. In this case, one is working with a structured development of the music in the film, however insignificant and weak it may be, justifying its value—particularly in a narrative sense—and attempting to communicate not only emotionally but also intellectually. Soundtracks that are not structured thematically but which respond to overall needs and are not merely sequential, seek to fulfil other ends. These are not narrative but have to do with ambience or emotion, and do not establish any intellectual communication with the audience.

5.1. Film scores with a thematic structure: The power pyramid

A soundtrack thematically structured is made up of themes placed in various parts of the film. These are applied with specific aims which fit in with repetitions, variations and with other themes of unequal importance and which perform different functions. If a soundtrack starts out to satisfy the general needs of the film, the musical theme looks after specific needs, such as a character, an idea, a sentiment—whatever factor that may be isolated and given musical emphasis. What is important is to understand the score as a whole and see the themes as its breakdown into hierarchical levels. This may be because of a quantitative importance (when one theme is used more frequently than another), a dramatic or narrative importance (when it is more necessary than the others), or simply a question of power. However, a theme is not more important because it is repeated more times but rather because it has greater dramatic and/or narrative weight in the music script.

Except when the soundtrack has only a single theme, the themes making up a structured soundtrack may be grouped in the following categories: initial theme, final theme, principal theme, central theme, secondary and sub-theme which, in some cases, may be the same. That is to say, an initial theme may also be a final or central theme, or there may be more than one central or secondary theme. In addition, themes may co-exist with motifs or fragments. Each of these categories has various tasks, so that themes of great dramatic or narrative importance are able to co-exist with others that have a merely circumstantial usefulness. In order that the entire musical structure (sometimes quite complex) might fit well together and have the greatest possible scope, it is fundamental to know how to coordinate all the themes in what we may call *The power pyramid*, which establishes the hierarchical and power relations between them.

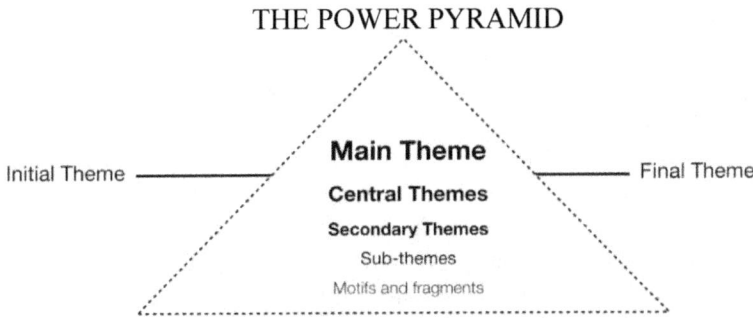

- **Central themes**

Before dealing with the main theme, we shall begin with central themes as the main theme is, in itself, a central theme. The central theme has an implication and a significance that must be understood by the spectator although this implication or significance may in fact change. A central theme takes on narrative responsibilities and for this reason is of prime importance. As it is generally used in various parts of the music script, its meaning must be clearly understood, if not, the theme is absolutely useless. The central theme exists in order to give life to something important in the form of music—a character (or several characters), a concept or whatever element that needs to be defined. If a central theme is applied to a character, it helps to explain the character and, starting out from this first explanation, all that is needed is to play the theme again to show how he/she might be feeling. The same thing happens when the theme refers to an emotion or a specific sensation (love, hate, etc.) or to a concept (freedom, bravery, honour). Its presence makes it possible to provide the literary script with a reference (from the music script) that will cite, complement, amplify, deepen, alter or even contradict what is explicit or suggested in the literary script.

If you want to refer to a character, an emotion or a concept through music, there is no better way to do this than to assign it a central theme. If this link is established, it will not be necessary for all of this to be explained in the literary script. It will be enough to use this theme to explain things which, as well as clarifying, will reduce the narrative burden carried by the literary script. For this reason, it is important that a central theme be sufficiently well developed so that this communication with the audience be efficient, not only in emotional terms but especially in a narrative sense. At this point we should mention the central theme's genetic code or DNA, which is its very essence. Consider, for example, how we might define a sentiment by music. Romantic music for two people in love may not be enough if there is something deeper or more difficult to express in the amorous relationship. What kind of romanticism should we make use of? Optimistic romanticism... melancholic... a romanticism more dramatic or even fatalistic? It is absolutely essential that the central theme's genetic code be sufficiently well defined at its dramatic level, in order to clarify and not confuse and to be able to focus on how we want the audience to see the character or understand the emotion or concept. As was pointed out right from the beginning, the music always imposes itself. Unless nothing more is intended than something generic, it is important to make use of integrated music for creating a central theme. When the most specific elements of a character, an emotion or a concept are carried by the central theme, whatever it is will be better understood. Furthermore, this will establish its basic dramatic level, which can then be maintained or changed if necessary throughout the music script. If the central theme is to be shared, it is important to include only those elements that are common to the characters that share them. Otherwise, if we assign to one of the characters some characteristic or facet which they do not possess (for example, if one is optimistic and the other pessimistic), to include pessimism as a factor in the genetic code of this shared central theme would automatically attribute this to the optimistic character as well. This also happens with collective central themes. In order to create a collective centre theme, it is necessary to draw up a common DNA which will serve for the entire group and not impose characteristics that only part of the collective possesses.

In *Unforgiven* (Clint Eastwood, 1992), the central theme, which the director himself wrote to apply to the surly character he personally would play, underlines his melancholy character and his need for redemption in a clear and simple way while still showing him as capable of gentleness. As a result, certain elements are made to stand out above his apparent unpleasantness and hardness. The music lodges right within the character to bring out those characteristics in the form of music and display them to the audience. The protagonist of *Papillon* (Franklin J. Schaffner, 1973) has only one goal—to regain his lost freedom after being condemned to forced labour for life in a French Guyana prison. For this two and a half hour film, Jerry Goldsmith wrote a brief score focussed on the theme of freedom. This melody took shape as the film developed, beginning with a sad and beaten tone only to reach its fullness when the victim finally manages to escape, at which point it sounded open and free of any melancholy. It was not the character's theme but of his yearning and the reason he was able to keep fighting against his hostile environment. And that was made clear to the audience through the music.

The life of the two protagonists (the butler and the housekeeper) in *The Remains of the Day* (James Ivory, 1993) shows up through their daily routine and becomes nothing more than devoting themselves to the people they service until with the passing of the years they realize that they have not lived their own lives at all. The music by Richard Robbins precisely explains all the monotony in which they have lived their methodical lives. This is not music for the characters but for the concept applied to both characters and is thus shared. It is like the central theme John Williams wrote for *Close Encounters of the Third Kind*, which was not a theme for a character but for a shared concept I am referring to what we could call a *theme of attraction*, something with a strong hypnotic power over the characters as well as over the audience. It is a hypnotizing effect that leads to Devil's Mountain. The hypnosis begins from the moment when the protagonist is touched by extraterrestrial light and is heard almost imperceptibly when he turns on the radio following his first encounter and also in all the news about the first contacts people have with the extraterrestrial situation. It works like a snake-charmer providing more and more clues to reach exactly where the music leads you, working all through the film at different intensities and rhythms, from different instruments, but always with the same intention. This is music that progressively opens a pathway, a physical road toward the protagonists' final destiny and, as we come closer to Devil's Mountain, grows incessantly more powerful and insistent.[21] Just as the music becomes more and more clearly defined, going from brief chords and motifs until it develops into a powerful, almost obsessive theme, it no longer makes sense when the protagonists arrive to where it has led them. It finally disappears, giving place to another theme that has been developing—the communication theme—the five notes in diegesis—which become an incidental theme that we talked about earlier in the section on diegesis.

The very importance of a central theme means that there should only be a limited number of them, otherwise there will be a risk of confusion. A film with ten central themes would be managing ten different concepts and keeping all these different variations in mind would make it virtually impossible to assimilate. This implies that we must select what is to be emphasized by central themes and what should be avoided or relegated to secondary roles. Imagine if in the case of a version of the Gospel according to St. Mark, for example, we were to apply thirteen central themes (one for each apostle and another for Jesus Christ). The result would be so confusing that the music would end up being an impediment to understanding the film. Not even if it lasted for fifteen hours and was fully explained could the music go so far. It would demand too much attention and would not work. On the other hand, logic would suggest that we write two

---

[21] It is enough to remember the scene in which Roy—who is making a reproduction of Devil's Mountain in clay and is troubled because he does not understand why he needs to make it—goes into the garden and asks the Heavens what is happening to him. In answer, the Heavens give him the theme of attraction.

central themes or perhaps three, one for Jesus Christ and others for Judas Escariot, Peter and James and nothing for the rest. This would be a natural choice. It is obvious that not all central themes applied to a music script are equally important. Some are more relevant and others less so. Some are very powerful. The most important of them all is the main theme.

- **Main theme**

The main theme is a central theme and as such it has all the characteristics set out above. It is a main theme because of all the central themes it is the most important. In the world of the music script, the main theme is king while the central themes are the princes.

How do you make a central theme the main theme? Not from the number of times it is used seeing that a central theme may occur more often than the main theme. Nor should we take into consideration a greater degree of acceptance by the public although sometimes it may coincide. A central theme may be very popular and still be less substantial than others in the music script. In *The Godfather*, for example, the Sicily theme (wrongly termed the *Love Theme* since this was not its task) is the better known and the one that had the greatest popular success. Nevertheless, among the central themes it is the least important in narrative or dramatic terms. It was inserted in the Sicily sequences and was based on a variation of a theme that Nino Rota himself wrote for *Fortunella* (Eduardo De Filippo, 1958). It is a beautiful melody, quite melancholic, that we hear for the first time over the pensive face of Vito Corleone, in bed, and is gently linked with the bucolic image of Michael Corleone walking in the mountains of Sicily and later on during his walk toward his family's town. At first it is related to the falling in love and later marriage of Michael and Apollonia. However, its use in this film and in the sequel *The Godfather, Part II* (Francis Ford Coppola, 1974) links it to the relationship of the Corleone family with their place of origin, Sicily. It was the central theme that won the most commercial success but its participation in the film is limited and circumstantial compared with the other two central themes, that of Michael Corleone and that of the Padrino, which is the main theme.

The central theme for Michael Corleone is slow, languid and romantic and develops parallel to the evolution of the character. It comes in following Sollozo's attack on Don Vito Corleone coinciding with Michael's growing role in the family's activities, which give him preeminent status. While it is his brother Santino who takes over the reins while the patriarch is convalescing, the audience already knows on whom the direction of the family will fall, given that neither Santino himself nor the lawyer Tom Hagen nor the other brother Fredo have a musical theme of their own. Because of its evolution and its narrative involvement, this central theme is much more important than the central Sicily theme, despite its having little popular or commercial success. However, while it was significant, this theme did not turn out to be the main one. The main theme was reserved for the Godfather, the Padrino himself. In the form of a waltz, this theme associates the authority of the patriarch—not of the character but of the institution—with status and power. It makes its first appearance played slowly by a solo trumpeter along with the Paramount symbol and continues up to the initial sequence of the film and is always heard linked to the figure of the Padrino in scenes of violence or in family scenes. Its designation as the main theme is established when it replaces that of Michael when he takes over the position as the new Padrino of the family and, by inheriting its music, renounces his own. The main theme is much more important than the central theme and yet appears fewer times.

What determines the nature of the main theme is the dramatic or narrative strength it holds in the soundtrack as a whole—its overall role in the music script, which is the axis around which the other themes move. In other words, it is the most significant reference—the spine of the film, in musical terms. Because of this, we should take care in considering more than one of the central themes the main one, as that would mean giving them equal status which they do not have. On the other hand, being sure which theme is going to be the main theme, helps to define the narrative strategy for the construction of the music script—the perspective from which the film is to be seen and structured. To say, for example, that the three central themes set out in *The Godfather* are main themes is to put them on an equal plane, which is neither true nor fair. It undervalues the main theme and gives too much value to the other central themes. They are not equal and, because of this, cannot be considered in the same way.

How many main themes are there in *Star Wars, Episode V – The Empire Strikes Back* (Irving Kershner, 1980)? Really only one — the heroic fanfare (the so-called *Star Wars Theme*), which is the film's most significant and powerful theme and carries the film's real message. In significance and symbolism it stands well above the themes of the Princess Leia, of Darth Vader, of Yoda or of any other theme in John Williams' soundtrack. To maintain that along with this fanfare, the Darth Vader theme is also a main theme would be to consider them equally significant, something that is quite clearly not the case and that would be confusing for the audience, given that the reference the main theme brings to the music script as a whole would then be lost.

In *Braveheart* (Mel Gibson, 1995) with music by James Horner there are a number of central themes. Three of the most important are dealt with below:

1.– Central love theme. This is the protagonist William Wallace's theme of unconditional love for his beloved Murron, who is murdered. It begins tentatively with Murron as a child attending the funeral of William Wallace's father and brother. When she plucks a flower and hands it to William the theme becomes stronger indicating that something is beginning which will determine part of the protagonist's story. When they meet again years later after William returns home the theme comes in again although still in a prudent manner, as the relationship is just beginning. Nevertheless, later on when William gives the flower back to Murron it takes on more significance. It sounds more strongly when he proposes matrimony. However, shortly after the wedding she is killed by English soldiers. The theme does not disappear there but to some extent Wallace takes it on. When he moves in to kiss his dead wife we hear some slight notes from the theme as if it was about to disappear with her. But after the kiss it sounds louder now in full possession of Wallace and from this moment on the theme turns into the musical materialization of the memory of Murron, of pure love, of strength and the shield Wallace will use to deal with what lies ahead. At times when it occurs, it stands at the spatial reference level putting Murron or her memory in the scene. On other occasions, however, it comes in without any apparent reason and without making any reference to her, as is the case when Wallace has his first encounter with the princess. In principle, the theme is used to make reference to Murron seeing that Wallace talks of her. But the princess Isabelle, falls in love with him and the use of the central theme indicates the beginning of that sentiment in her and, after that, the theme is heard each time they meet. Nevertheless, never at any moment does use of this theme suggest that Wallace has fallen in love again. For him, Murron is the one and only. However, the theme is contagious and takes hold of the princess because she loves him. When at the end of the film the hero is booed by the crowd before facing what will be a brutal death, the memory of Murron becomes even stronger and this is the last time the theme is heard.

2.– Central theme for William Wallace. This other theme, of an epic nature, has the purpose of showing the hero, his conviction and his faith with which he will imbue the men who will fight on his side. The first appearance of the theme is subtle: William is still a child and declares to his father that he is well able to fight. The second time it is heard is much later, at the beginning of the battle of Stirling, while the protagonist advances exultant among the Scottish troops. But it is not until the battle is won when it can be noted in a totally developed form. Toward the end of the film it is heard on two occasions. The first time is before the betrayal that takes Wallace to his disgraceful end. He has been tricked and, not suspecting such betrayal, believes that finally an accord has been reached with the Scottish nobles. Now his theme sounds epic and spreads optimism, underlining his ingenuousness in the situation. Finally, the last and powerful appearance of the theme is while he is being tortured when William takes one last breath and proclaims freedom for his country. It is at this moment that the theme comes in at its fullest. And then, along with him, it dies.

3.– Central theme of the Homeland. It refers to Scotland and stands at the narrative level of the land with the bag-pipes playing an especially important role. The theme is melancholy and sad, although it also sounds solemn and sometimes even spirited in some scenes. Its use in the battle of Stirling is significant—when the Scottish soldiers hold firm against the English cavalry, we hear bag-pipes playing against the English drums. Both carry on their own particular blow-by-blow struggle increasing in intensity as the two sides come closer and closer. However, the musical battle is resolved before the narrative and the music of the English ends up dominating that of the Scots. This theme fluctuates between optimism and pessimism according to the situation of the Scottish patriotic struggle. The last time it comes in is at the end of the film following the death of Wallace at the moment when Robert Bruce, accompanied by the Scottish troops, marches off to pay homage to England. Because the image being shown is that of a beaten Scotland, the theme sounds sad, solemn and melancholy. But, when Robert Bruce changes his mind and decides to fight, the theme recovers and again becomes powerful.

These are the three most notable central themes in *Braveheart* and, although there are others, they are not as important. These three, however, are of special significance because of what they represent and signify in the development of the film. These themes raise a number of questions: are they exactly of equal importance? What is the spinal column that holds the film together? Is this a love story, a memoir, an homage to an historical figure, or is it pure patriotic sentiment? The feelings of a character, either in principle or logically, will always lie below what the character represents, and more so if he is a national hero like William Wallace. Because of this it is not possible to give equal status to the music for his sentiments with that for his role as hero. Nor can we compare those sentiments with the sense of a Scottish homeland, because this is not an individual sentiment but a collective one. Therefore, the central love theme, without losing its significance, will be of less importance than the two other themes, because *Braveheart* is not essentially a love story.

The difficulty lies in deciding on the key figure here—William Wallace or Scotland. Either option would have its own logic: if the main theme were to be that of William Wallace it would make sense because the film is about him and he is the protagonist; if it were the struggle of the people as a whole for Scottish independence, this could be explained by the fact that the homeland always comes before its heroes, and William Wallace fought for something bigger than himself. And this last option is exactly what ends up as most important, although with nuances. In the final scene already mentioned, when William Wallace has died and Robert Bruce decides to fight, what is heard in full splendour is the Scotland theme, the absolute sovereign and definitive message of the music script. It does, however, show its generosity by including the William Wallace theme in its melody at the spatial level of its references as a tribute and homage to his person. The combination of the two themes does not take place on a level of absolute equality. It is obvious that the homeland (Scotland) continues on and that it pays tribute to its hero. However, the hero is dead and the homeland still alive. The William Wallace theme cannot remain over the scene and the film's grand message is transmitted to the audience by the main theme. Of course, this interpretation may be challenged by the strong arguments in favour of maintaining the Wallace theme as the film's main theme. Who or what is finally designated to take on the category of main theme is of prime importance, as the argument and viewpoint of the film can turn out notably different depending on the perspective taken. What is not acceptable is to give them both an identical importance because doing this will dilute the film's message.

Obviously, there may be situations in which the two central themes serve as main themes but always when it is quite impossible to establish any hierarchy. This is the case when we have a character with a double personality (a kind of Jekyll and Hyde) and when neither of these two personalities is stronger than the other. Where each of these personalities is written as a central theme and there is no indication from the music that, even in any untold future in the literary script, the duel will be resolved in favour of one or the other, we might consider them both as main themes. However, it is imperative that there not be the slightest indication or suggestion of the victory of one theme over the other. Should it exist, we would not have a situation with two main themes but with a main theme (the victor) and a central theme. Not only would it not be logical to view them as equal, but it would be a major error to deal with them as if they were, because instead of clarifying this would only confuse.

Generally it is not specially complicated to decide which is the main theme in a soundtrack. James Bernard's music for *Dracula* (Terence Fisher, 1958) and that by John Williams for *Dracula* (John Badham, 1979) both have a Gothic quality in common in their main themes, written not so much for the vampire character as for his enormous power. In the first case, the main theme puts emphasis on the most terrifying and decadent aspects, while Williams, picking up on these, deals more with the romantic and the seductive elements. In spite of the abundant music in both films, it is not difficult to understand that the main themes are those led by the music script and that the other themes remain subordinate to them. *Body Heat* (Lawrence Kasdan, 1981), with music by John Barry, is a remake of *Double Indemnity* and tells the story of a woman who seduces a man and incites him to kill her husband with fatal consequences for the uncautious lover. The composer wrote a main theme not applied to either character but rather about their sexual passion. In this melody there is warmth and a tremendous sensuality, adequate to the protagonists' desire and ardour. However, the characters cannot be considered equal either in who they are nor in their intentions: she sets a trap and he falls into it. For this reason, an element of mystery was added to the music making the main theme seductive while at the same time creating a definite sense of uncertainty. While placed at the spatial level of emotion—of the characters and also of the audience—the music had a different dramatic level, seen from the point of view of one or the other character. With her, the music is pure trickery; with him, absolute passion. Such was its importance that it relegated a minor role to the rest of the themes. Naturally, if a film has an important protagonist who is assigned a musical theme, it is quite likely that this will be the main theme, unless he is given another one. If the film moves around an emotion or a concept, in musical terms that emotion or concept will certainly be the main theme. There are very few forked backbones in music scripts. To freely assign such a status to central themes that are not equal diverts the focus of attention around which the music script evolves, both in its interpretation and especially in its construction.

- **Counter-theme**

The counter-theme is a central theme and as such serves to establish something in the form of music. Nevertheless, it is a specific kind of central theme whose purpose is to contradict or oppose whatever other central theme it might encounter. For although it complements its own needs its main purpose is to confront another central theme. If there is no struggle between a central theme and a counter-theme, it means there is no real counter-theme but only another central theme. The main purpose of a counter-theme is to add struggle or conflict to the music, thereby magnifying it—pitting good against evil, friendship against hatred, life against death—opposing concepts which so often appear in the storyline. Counter-themes ensure that the audience be not only aware of a particular conflict but that they also perceive it in the music, thus giving it even more importance. It is therefore up to the composer to make sure that the confrontation in the storyline is present as well in the music through the use of a counter-theme.

The counter-theme does not have to join in the theme it opposes. Its mere presence enriches it. A central theme that, for example, expresses nobility, becomes even nobler if placed up against another theme reflecting villainy. In *The Magnificent Seven* (John Sturges, 1960), Elmer Bernstein wrote a fanfare dedicated to the seven protagonists who are fighting to save a Mexican town from the oppression of a group of gangsters. This festive, lively and happy melody represented the positive concepts of good, of friendship, of life itself. With this music the spectator could well understand the values that the characters represented. Against this, however, he inserted a counter-theme—absolutely opposed to the earlier theme— which he applied to the villains. Written as a march with a syncopated rhythm and a constant repetition of eight low notes that coincided with the violent character of the gangsters, this theme embodied evil, hatred, death—the very opposite of those earlier values. The fact that Bernstein used a theme and a counter-theme (both of them used quite frequently) helped make clear that the big duel, which would take place at the end of the film, had been there right from the beginning. Although the heroes and villains do not meet until the final scene, the confrontation set earlier by the music makes it possible for the audience to perceive that struggle before it ever takes place. This is an enormously positive result of the early creation of tension.

Another example is to be found in *Star Wars* although the counter-theme appears only in *The Empire Strikes Back*. John Williams had written the famous fanfare which would be the main theme. As in *The Magnificent Seven*, it is a powerful melody that transmits positive values (again, these are of goodness, friendship, life, etc.). For *The Empire Strikes Back* he composed a theme for Darth Vader, giving him a counter-theme of solemn and syncopated music, which expressed quite contrary sentiments (evil, hatred, death) to the main theme. There is also a counter-theme in the trilogy begun in *The Lord of the Rings: The Fellowship of the Ring* (Peter Jackson, 2001) with music by Howard Shore and in *Star Trek* (J.J. Abrams,

2009) with a soundtrack by Michael Giacchino, as well as in many films where it is desired to magnify or solemnize some kind of conflict. But this conflict—and it is important to emphasize this point—does not refer exclusively to what is common in epic or sensational films, but can appear in films of an intimate or dramatic nature. It is enough that there be something to confront musically.

Where a conflict exists between a counter-theme and a central theme, there must be a resolution in favour or one of the other or even acceptance of a draw between them. For once this musical duel begins it must lead somewhere otherwise there would be no point to having used it. A counter-theme can destroy a central theme, taking away its sense and significance, greatly reducing it and even taking its place. In a kind of musical coup, it can assume the position of main theme and even set itself up as king of the themes right from the start. If this is not the case, it will be no more than a threat that finally peters out or succumbs to the theme or themes confronting it. All these options make up some of the dramatic and narrative possibilities that can be achieved through use of a counter-theme. Some examples of this:

In *The Omen*, with music by Jerry Goldsmith, the coral theme *Ave Satani* is the main theme of the film, the music used to explain the various degrees of the Devil's fury. It is the main theme because it does not meet any resistance and right to the end of the film maintains its power intact. But is it also a counter-theme? Yes it is, and for just one reason, because there is a central theme which it attacks and destroys, a fragile and delicate melody applied as a reference for the sentiments of the father toward his family. It is, indeed, a struggle with a big difference in the strength of the themes involved. Therefore, faced with the steamroller power of the sinister main theme, the central theme can do nothing. It is thanks to this duel that the significance of both themes comes to the fore. If there had not been a struggle neither would there have been any comparisons.

We also find this in the animated film *Coraline* (Henry Selik, 2009) with music by Bruno Coulais. This animated film, dark and sinister, with its double storyline, is hardly conventional. There is the real world, that of Coraline and the world of the false mother. The child Coraline flees her own world to go into the other, which is a version apparently better than the first but where something very sinister awaits her. The music script is constructed on this duality with two grand themes—the main theme and the counter-theme.

The main theme is Coraline's theme while the counter-theme, that of the 'other' mother, is also the theme of the other world. The main theme is simple and very beautiful with a gentle, melancholy melody, sung by a pure voice transmitting innocence. It is applied to the real world and not to the fictitious one. This is significant as it implies that Coraline will lose her music in a territory not her own. It is the mother's music that invades this space. This counter-theme is a soft and penetrating melody, with fragments also interpreted by a pure voice, transmitting anguish and distrust. While the story and the images show a world and a mother that are perfect, the music reveals that all is not what it seems. The struggle between the false mother and the child also shifts to their music as each fights to occupy the space. The counter-theme is very invasive but finally the main theme ends the battle victorious.[22]

The point of departure in *The Untouchables* is the presentation of the counter-theme from Ennio Morricone's soundtrack. This serious and obsessive melody represents the power of the Mafia, but finally it can do little to prejudice the euphoric music of the main theme, applied to Elliot Ness and his group of untouchables. It can happen, of course, that a central theme takes on the role of counter-theme as the film evolves, but never right at the beginning. The film presents its central themes and it so happens that one of these turns out to be a counter-theme, as we see in *La vita è bella*. Nicola Piovani's music for this film revolves around two central themes: one happy and the other romantic, which respectively express the vitality of the protagonist and his love for his wife. The film is divided into three parts—one comic, another tragic (in the concentration camp) while the epilogue—a counter-theme is heard representing the Nazi horror. This shows up in the first half as a warning but is heard in all its macabre splendour in the second part, although it will finally be overcome by the two positive themes which furthermore outlive it.

---

[22] This struggle starts right from the beginning of the film in the opening credits where we hear a mix of the two themes, to later on separate giving place to the main theme and the counter-theme.

Other examples are to be found in *Gladiator* where the counter-theme that Hans Zimmer applies to the Emperor Commodus confronts the other two central themes—that of the hero and that of Maximus, the man who embodies that hero—and, as we have already explained, does so from a radically opposite position. Or in *Taxi Driver* (Martin Scorsese, 1976) for which Bernard Herrmann composed the music, in which the duel theme/counter-theme begins right at the start of the film, is maintained throughout and ends up providing three consecutive endings, as we shall discover later. We find the same duel between themes in Steven Spielberg's films—*Close Encounters of the Third Kind*, *E.T. The Extra-Terrestrial* and *Catch Me If You Can*, with scores by John Williams. In *Close Encounters of the Third Kind* there is the music for the army, which acts as counterpoint to the other themes. In *E.T. The Extra-Terrestrial* the music associated with the adults struggles against the music for the extraterrestrial and the theme for his friendship with the child. In the magnificent final part of the film, all these themes confront each other in a fight for survival. From the moment the scientists lose E.T. (when Michael and Elliott take him to the forest in a van), the counter-theme appears like a raging beast in all its fury. In a pitched battle where it attempts to sabotage the other themes with an obvious lack of control, which is very carefully orchestrated and leads to the last stage of the film. In *Catch Me If You Can*, the music also chases itself like in a cat-and-mouse game with a fight theme/counter-theme but in a dramatic sense. This adventure comedy with touches of cops-and-robbers suspense neither has, nor does it pretend to have, an especially complicated or sophisticated soundtrack. As the film tells the story of an impostor, someone who changes his identity time after time while always remaining the same person, the melodies change their timbre but maintain their essence. There is a main theme (that of Frank) and two central themes—the chase theme and the theme of the father.

The main theme is heard in various occasions always reflecting the mood of the character. Jovial, fresh and vital, it gives off a certain innocence always describing the character's little schemes and the emotion he feels as he prepares them or delightedly observes their results. This is the music of his longings, of the happy world he wants to live in to escape from his difficult family situation. His contagious joy shows reality from his point of view, which puts the spectator on his side emotionally without seeing what he does as reproachable. In

5. Distribution of Music

short, these are the music's main characteristics: 1.- it is expansive as it inundates the space around Frank and is transmitted to other characters; 2. - it is capable of silencing other themes: as Frank prepares to make himself pass off as an aircraft pilot, he writes to his father. Instead of our hearing the father's theme, as would be logical, the Frank theme continues to be heard—the young man's dream is more powerful than his nostalgia, and the same thing happens when he decides to pass himself off as a doctor. 3.- it enters into other people as well: when the superiors of Carl (the police) consider Frank's case as a lost cause, we see him sitting pensive at a table covered with checks, wondering how find a way to trap the swindler. At that moment instead of the chase theme we hear a secondary theme, one of suspense, which reflects the policeman's confusion. Very subtly, a few notes of the Frank theme are slipped in and, in this way, the music indicates that he is trying to put himself in Frank's place, to think like him and be able to figure out his movements and thus trap him.[23] 4. - it continues through the chase and only when Frank is apprehended does the chase theme die (Carl is no longer a threat), while the Frank theme is maintained. From that moment on the music stops representing the ideal but unreal world the young man had constructed around himself, to take him into another life, honest and full of hope, where Frank will use his talents for more noble causes. There is just one moment of conflict in all this, when Frank is in the street, while we are still hearing his theme, and the vision of a pilot's uniform tempts him into escaping into his dream world again. But other than in that scene, the music symbolizes his redemption from past errors and his subsequent success in life. This idea is fully realized in the closing credits when the entire orchestra, with tremendous impetus, plays the main theme for the last time.

The first counter-theme is the chase theme. Written in a progressive jazz style it is dynamic and denotes tension with something of menace, although it falls short of being dramatic. It

---

[23] At this point we hear a theme without any specific melody, which suggests that nothing is very clear to Carl, that he does not know how to resolve the puzzle. In the following scene he talks to experts about printing checks and the scene continues without the theme we are hearing being recognizable. But when the experts mention France, Carl finds the clue he has been looking for and, at that moment, we hear the chase theme.

comes up for the first time accompanying the greater part of the film's opening credits. In its rapid and fleeting notes the idea of flight is contained in a very visual way.[24] When Carl is close to Frank or discovers new ways to capture him, we hear brief notes of this counter-theme and in this way the concept of chase is reaffirmed at the spatial level of references. However, it does not manage take away the power of the main theme. Its reduction to a fragment weakens it against Frank's theme and, furthermore, it will never enjoy that theme's expansive strength but will be limited always to accompanying the same specific act without ever changing its meaning. When Frank is finally captured the theme will die.

As counterpoint to the joy of the main theme there is the father's theme, more downcast and melancholy. This, too, is a counter-theme, although with dramatic pretensions, and throughout the film it keeps changing its meaning. It begins representing Mr. Abagnale's hurt dignity to then become a bond of union with his son, symbolizing the nostalgia Frank feels for his father while momentarily taking him back to the crude reality from which he escaped. When the father dies, the theme survives in the form of a memory in Frank's mind who finds himself (working for the FBI) in a situation that is saddening for him and very similar to that which his father experienced in the past. The music establishes an emotional parallel between the two situations while at the same time tightening the links between them. Thus, a theme that initially reflected a specific sensation of one of the characters widens its meaning, affecting the protagonist and extending far beyond the death of the character it represents. It works as a counter-theme while producing the contrast between the joy in the main theme and the bitterness of the counter-theme. It does, however, stop being a counter-theme when the son recovers it following the death of his father, and uses it to evoke him.

---

[24] Its principal motif, very short and recognizable—in three parts, the first two of just four notes—is always repeated twice as if one was chasing the other. At times, this repetition of the motif is in turn followed by another two repetitions interpreted by a new instrument. As if this was not enough, this little game with the principal motif is followed at times by a brief interlude where one instrument plays a series of notes and another responds with several others. This happens three or four times as if the first were running away with the second in pursuit. The effect is reinforced by the integration of clicks of the fingers (immediacy and rapid reflexes) along with calls for silence (shhh!) pronounced vocally (secrets and confidences).

- **Secondary themes**

Central themes are important, both dramatically and in a narrative sense, while secondary themes do not have the same significance although they may be more often used. They do not take on narrative responsibility, do not assume any implication or significance that must be understood by the spectator and as they do not define anything, there can be as many as are needed without limit. Their usefulness depends on circumstances. Once a secondary theme has been applied, no one expects the audience to retain it and therefore it will be rapidly taken over by the music that follows it. Because secondary themes lack narrative or informative content, they do not provide anything intellectually but only emotionally, whereas a central theme may link not only emotionally but also intellectually.

Secondary themes are used for specific resolutions in particular sequences. In a car chase, for instance, the music adds dynamism, momentum, and rhythm, but once it is over, it might well be forgotten. Of course, a secondary theme can be used again as often as wanted or needed, so long as the circumstances are identical or at least very similar and continue to be so. If a secondary theme should be reused in different circumstances or contexts, it might acquire some significance for the audience who might then confuse it with a central theme; there must be a dramatic or narrative reason that explains or justifies its presence in different contexts. Because of this, secondary themes must always take up their space in the film with a definite meaning and be clearly justified. Of itself, a secondary theme is incapable of measuring up to a central theme in either strength or importance. However, uniting several or many of them at the same dramatic level may indeed take on a determining role, though they will continue to remain secondary themes.[25] Joining secondary themes at the same dramatic level (that of the threat, for example) is a powerful tool not to be overlooked which, furthermore, may be very useful especially when it is not intended to give these themes a concrete meaning. If James Newton Howard, for example, had referenced the threat from the forest in *The Village* in the form of a

---

[25] Put another way, if this might be permitted: an orc (one of the beasts in The Lord of the Rings) is very easily vanquished. However, 20,000 of them together are frightening.

central theme, the audience would have a definition of the threat in the form of music. However, what is heard from the forest is not just one music but many, insignificant when considered individually but quite substantial taken together under the same dramatic level. They do not define but they manage to disconcert. For this reason, secondary themes are not always just *fillers* although they often fulfil that role. They are also important if one is trying to avoid making explicit certain ideas or concepts.

- **Initial theme**

The initial theme is that which goes with the opening credits of the film. It is not necessarily the one which opens the film nor the one we first hear. If the title credits are preceded by a scene with music, this music would not be the initial theme unless, beginning before the credits, it then it extended to these. In all the James Bond film series, for example, we find first sequences accompanied by music that later leads into the credits where we hear the initial theme in the form of a song. The prior music would only be an initial theme if the same music were to be maintained during the credits, which does not happen in James Bond films. It may occur that a film does not have an initial theme, if the credits carry no music or if there are no credits at the beginning. Of course, an initial theme may be the union of more than one musical theme, which later on in the film evolve differently. They are of paramount importance and can take on different roles although, it must be said, an initial theme applied over title credits in black, where there is no action at all, is not the same as when it is over credits where some action is taking place. It can also happen that there are opening credits where we see only the logo of the production company and the title of the film but nothing more. Here, the music would be the initial theme.

Generically, its most useful and most basic value is to help present the film, both aesthetically and stylistically, to the audience: a romantic initial theme, for instance, that presents a film that is going to be romantic or a terrifying melody that introduces a story of terror. Just remember the placid beginning of the film *Life of Pi* (Ang Lee, 2012) thanks to the nice initial theme by Mychael Danna. Nevertheless, the initial titles of a film (and more so if these come over a black background and are therefore without any narrative action) form a privileged space to do something more interesting than merely inserting an initial theme for aesthetic reasons.

An initial theme can definitely condition how an audience enters into a film, long before it is fully laid out. If the initial theme, for example, is an extremely moving romantic melody, the audience will deduce that what they are going to see is about a dramatic romance. Even though the literary script does not bring in the tragedy until well into the story, the music will have opened the way and thus the audience will be waiting for it. This is, of course, a deliberate ploy to give the audience clues that are not shown in the literary script. If, on the other hand, the initial theme is romantic—sweet and agreeable—the audience will slip into the film with the same innocence (and lack of knowledge) as the characters, and will have to deal with the tragedy when it comes in the literary script. Both possibilities are valid but provide different results. It all depends on the choice of the initial theme and knowing, as we have said from the beginning, that the audience does not question what the music is saying. Even if the tragedy does not happen until the final sequence of the film (and even though the protagonists are constantly accompanied by sweet music) the audience will have its doubts about their ongoing happiness if, in the initial theme, they have been given that specific indication. In *Fargo* (Joel Coen, 1996), for example, the imposing initial theme moves the tragedy ahead over images that seem peaceful enough (a car travelling along a road).

It can become even more significant, as happens in two fairly similar films, such as *Spartacus* and *The Fall of the Roman Empire* (Anthony Mann, 1964). Both films are located in the same environment (Imperial Rome). The context in both is one of great violence (rebellion and war) and, in each of them, a love story blossoms or tries to survive (of Spartacus and Varinia, and of Livius and Lucilla). Nevertheless, the way each film begins is different. In *Spartacus*, the initial theme by Alex North is a theme of violence, chaos, disorder, conflict and this is the context with which the spectator begins. Later on, as the film develops, love comes in (with its musical theme) but it has to start from scratch, as does the audience. In *The Fall of the Roman Empire*, Dimitri Tiomkin wrote an initial theme that was entirely romantic so that the spectator began watching the film where the conflict was not going to be the axis but the love between the protagonists. Furthermore, this initial theme was especially relevant for stressing the sadness in a love that was condemned right from the start because of the fatally hostile environment. It is true that in Anthony Mann's film the sentimental relations between the protagonists is not created but already exists right from the start whereas in Kubrick's film this relationship has to be built. Simply as an hypothesis, let us imagine a change in the romantic themes of both these films. In *Spartacus* we make the initial theme the romantic theme and in the credits for *The Fall of the Roman Empire* we put any of the violent themes (of which there are many) that Tiomkin wrote. The effect would be the same but exactly the reverse. There would be many violent war scenes but (in the case of *Spartacus*) the spectator would always be waiting for love to show up while, in our adjusted version of *The Fall of the Roman Empire*, the audience would move into a violent and chaotic world where, like a flower in the desert, love would make its appearance. In this way, the initial theme can determine how the spectator enters into the picture.

We have considered the initial theme as an aesthetic element or as a determining factor directing the spectator toward something specific. But there are other options: the initial theme could be used as an indication of what is going to happen, as a warning or a point of connection with a later scene. This is what happens in many Alfred Hitchcock films with music by Bernard Herrmann and keeps showing up in all of those that have followed the narrative method of this brilliant New York composer. He takes advantage of the opening credits (with no action) to indicate what is about to happen, presenting an initial theme that will be especially important in the film so that when it comes up for the first time in the film story the spectator remembers the music that came in with the opening credits. In this way he emphasizes its importance over other music used in the film. In *Vertigo*, the initial theme comes up again in a specific scene when Judy (Kim Novak) is at the hairdresser getting the final touches that will turn her finally into Madeleine. This is when the spiral that will take the protagonist towards hell really begins. This is the same spiral that was also announced graphically in the opening credits designed by Saul Bass. In *North by Northwest* (1959), the initial theme puts forward very clearly the idea of the chase and will be heard again when this chase really begins for the desperate protagonist when he tries not to be killed in the car where he was left drunk. In *Psycho*, the vibrant initial theme obviously serves to present what kind of film it will be. But it serves for more than that, giving the spectator a subtle and subliminal indication to remember this music, because later on, when it comes up again, it will signal that something important is going to happen from that point on. This theme is used again in the sequence where the protagonist, fleeing after the robbery, drives the car late at night in the pelting rain. At that moment, because of the repetition of the theme, the audience knows that what has to happen will soon take place. If this theme had not come in before, the scene would simply be viewed as a tense episode and very little else.

This narrative method makes it possible to establish an interesting and useful intellectual communication with the audience and facilitate the discourse the theme is going to have, if indeed it is used as a narrative factor and does not remain simply an initial theme. This very useful and efficient method has neither been done away with nor improved but has been constantly repeated and is still to be found in current films such as *Signs* (M. Night Shyamalan, 2002) and *Drag Me To Hell* (Sam Raimi, 2009). Both of these apply initial themes, which will also be main themes, presented as such in the opening credits and of enormous importance to the film. In this respect, it helps that the credits not appear with any action because if there were, the audience would pay attention to what was happening and would settle into the spatial level of the action or emotions, finding it difficult to be at the level of references. Furthermore, as the film has just begun, it is probable that there is no reference yet that can be explained by the music apart from what might already be known by the audience outside of the film (such as the nuptial march by Mendelsson which would indicate that the protagonists of the first scene had got married). There is, of course, the possibility of placing the initial theme at the fourth spatial level—that of music brought forward. In this sense, we have already commented on *The Silence of the Lambs* and the same thing happens in *One Flew Over the Cuckoo's Nest* or in *The Ghost Writer* (Roman Polanski, 2010).

As already indicated in another section, in *One Flew Over the Cuckoo's Nest* there is a double dramatic level in that the whole incidental score is linked to the idea of freedom (which is what the protagonists desire), whereas the diegetic expresses the concept of oppression. In the credits we see the countryside at sunrise and a car driving through it. Jack Nitzsche's initial theme is an American Indian melody but, if the film does not take place on an Indian reserve nor is the protagonist (Jack Nicholson) an American Indian. What sense then does it make for the initial theme to be an American Indian melody? Let us begin by clarifying the fact that the protagonist does not have any music of his own and there is a very good reason for this: he will not be given anything to shelter him and, thus, will be left much more alone and abandoned. Nevertheless, there is one character, Chief Bromden (Will Sampson), who is an American Indian and who, while secondary, is the person who finally gives the protagonist the freedom he so dearly wants, killing him out of pity after they had performed a lobotomy on him. It is this scene (the last in the film) where for the second and last time, we hear again the music we heard with the opening credits, now fully developed. As this is the music associated with freedom (a metaphor, in this case) and with who supplies it (the American Indian character), the fact that the film begins with this theme implies not only that the event is foretold but in addition gives it the fullest significance. If this had not been applied as the initial theme, the final sequence would not have such a powerful emotional charge and the theme would have been simply another piece of music, like so many others, in the film.

In the case of *The Ghost Writer*, with music by Alexandre Desplat, the initial theme is applied throughout the film and goes right to the end. As in he previous example, the music—when it is simply the initial theme—does not have the significance it will gain later when it comes to represent the power, presence and menace of an entity (the company) of which the protagonist will end up victim. In the scene for the credits one might easily be confused as to its significance. We see the protagonist travelling in a boat and the music (speeded up and mysterious) does not seem to have any other reason than to set the scene for mystery. However, later on this will become clear. What is important is that the film begins with this music, whose meaning the audience does not known and therefore does not consider it a direct threat for the protagonist, as later it will become. Bringing it forward from when it takes on this meaning gives it much more importance.

In both cases, the themes are also main themes in their respective music scripts. But can an initial theme also be the main theme of a film? Surprising as it might seem, the answer is no. An initial theme, as such, will never be a main theme because the hierarchies among the themes have not yet been established. Of course, it may become one during the film or at the end. The important thing is to know when. The initial theme of *One Flew Over the Cuckoo's Nest* becomes the main theme in the scene where it takes on its fullest sense. In *The Ghost Writer*, when it has already overcome the many obstacles and is reborn in the final part in all its splendor (and wickedness, because it is also a counter-theme). To attribute or understand an initial theme as a main theme, apart from making no sense, destroys the dramatic or narrative evolution that this theme may possess if, right at the start, we concede it maximum power. A main theme must gain that place and it does so in the evolution it shows through the development of the music script.

This way of using the initial theme as a starting point for its later involvement in the film has been used for a long time. Nevertheless, for a relatively short time, a new method has been incorporated that is turning out to be useful and interesting. This involves not presenting a more or less developed theme as an initial theme but just a fragment of it, nothing more than a few notes that function more as a code than a presentation of the theme itself. This happens when the opening credits are made up mainly of the production house logo, the film title and little else. It can be seen, for example, in *Gladiator*, *Inception* and in *How to Train Your Dragon*. This code is made up of merely a few identifying notes from what will be a developed theme but is, in itself, an initial theme as it accompanies the opening credits, short as they may be. The film *Gladiator* begins with a few notes from the counter-theme (the central theme of the Emperor Commodus) and not with either of the two themes allocated to the protagonist (the heroic and the dramatic). This makes sense because, as an information code, it transmits to the spectator the great danger the figure of the Emperor will turn out to be. The two themes applied to the protagonist (one for the gladiator, the hero, and the other for Maximus, the human being) are themes at a high perception level, to engage the spectator as much in the heroism as in the melancholy of the protagonist. The counter-theme of the Emperor Commodus, nevertheless, always flows at a low level of perception and works subtly providing great power to its proprietor.

This shows the importance of giving the early warning, presenting it as a code at the beginning of the film.[26]

In *Inception* we hear barely a few notes of what is to be the main theme as a warning and we will not hear it again until well beyond half an hour into the film, when we are told for the first time what totems are and what they are for. In *How to Train Your Dragon*, on the other hand, we hear a few notes of what will end up being the main theme of the soundtrack, the beautiful melody linking the boy and the dragon. As it is a matter of a relationship that develops from a mutual mistrust to a perfect union, it makes sense that this theme evolve in synchronicity, and here the composer John Powell launches this code in the initial theme because it supposes a first step (already advanced) in that relationship.

The initial theme, therefore, may be seen as a point of departure and a launching-pad into the body of the film in order to obtain the very best result. In film, of course, what begins has to come to an end and this is why we need a final theme.

- **Final theme**

The final theme is the one that ends the film but is not necessarily the last to be heard. This is the music that goes with the final credits. However, if no music is applied to these, it would not make the last music heard (in a previous sequence) the final theme. Of course, the final theme may begin before the final credits and be developed along with these. Many films end this way with a final sequence accompanied by music that continues when the picture goes to black and the credits are shown. There may be cases when a film has no final theme: if the credits are not backed by music or there are no final credits. A final theme's importance is primordial seeing that it closes the film and may contribute not only to give stylistic coherence to the film as a whole but may also resolve dramatic questions.

---

[26] This is a simple and sinuous theme played by different string and flute instruments that call to mind the hissing of a serpent and relates to conspiration, to the occult and evil. The reference to the serpent is not in vain, as throughout the film there are references to serpents and Commodus, in the way he moves and acts, reminds you of them.

Naturally, it sometimes has a neutral sense: it may be made up of a single musical theme or a succession of various themes. As opposed to what happens with the initial theme, a final theme can be the main theme because the film is over and the share of power between the themes has been established. The initial theme and the final theme may be different, identical or a variation of the same. If they are identical, what is produced is a balanced and symmetrical effect, a way of closing a film within one musical colour, maintaining coherence even when the themes that have been inserted in the film have nothing to do with the initial and final themes. This is what happens in *Sleuth* (Joseph L. Mankiewicz, 1972) with a score by John Addison. The delightful music for the opening credits is a great game in which the composer invites us to take part. When this game of tricks and perfect crimes is over, the composer ends this curious fiesta in the same way, even if more briefly.

There is a tendency, rather more common than desirable, to insert one or more songs as a final theme. This is usually due to commercial criteria unless the song is a version of some of the film's music themes as is the case of the famous *My Heart Will Go On*, in *Titanic* (James Cameron, 1997), which is a sung version of the main theme of the film. However, it very often happens that a song is not called for, because the space for the closing credits is the ideal place for a composer to supply a conclusion to what the music script has been developing. Unfortunately, it often happens that this privilege is not given to the film (certainly not to the composer) who is condemned to do a real balancing act so that his entire narrative discourse makes sense. And this does not always happen.

Bernard Herrmann pulled it off in *Taxi Driver* with results worthy of detailed comment. With his music (and also in his final theme) he was able to add not one but three different endings to the film. We mentioned before how in, the music script, a real theme/counter-theme struggle takes place right from the start as the initial theme brings together the two central themes over which the soundtrack evolves. Each of these enjoy full dramatic equality in total agreement with what is explained in the film's literary script. The character of the taxi-driver Travis Bickle (Robert De Niro) has a dual personality and the whole music script is constructed to show and underline this duality. It does this, sacrificing along the way whatever other music might distract the discourse initiated by the initial theme. There is thus no music for the other key characters (the young prostitute, the young girl working in the electoral office or the pimp) and not even for New York, the huge city that is omnipresent in Scorsese's film. All the music is focussed on Travis Bickle's Jekyll/Hyde duality: hot jazz, calm and empathetic played by a saxophone for the Travis/Jekyll; while Travis/Hyde comes in the form of a dissonant musical theme that is dreary and dark. With the opening credits in the literary script, we see the taxi-driver driving his car through the night in New York. Both themes are alternated in fragments, resulting in an initial theme that is not particularly harmonious and gives a hint of the protagonist's personality. It does so somewhat illogically--the menacing theme over shots of the city while the jazz theme is heard over Travis's face and eyes. Given that the initial theme is no more than a warning of all that is going to happen, it is inevitable that the message it transmits to the audience is that the danger lies in the city and that the taxi-driver is not a threat. Immediately, however, the composer moves to correct that impression because at the moment the protagonist gets out of his taxi and walks toward the company office the music that follows him, and thus that which refers to him, is the music of Hyde.

Once the opening credits are over and the initial theme is finished, the two themes separate and are not heard again until the end. In the process, they engage in a struggle for survival. All the music stands at the spatial level of the emotions of the character which will determine that, independently of what the literary script tells us, it is the music script that will clarify whether it is Jekyll or Hyde who is dominating the protagonist's personality. It is all done fairly easily. Both central themes come up in the early stages along with the voice-over of the character explaining how he feels and what he is thinking. And while the sound level drops at these moments the music is maintained at the audience's unconscious level of perception so that the association of the music reaffirms the protagonist's thoughts.

The jazz theme will appear in his positive thoughts and situations: for example, when he gets a date with Betsy (Cybill Shepherd) or in his dealings with Iris (Jodie Foster), aware that he can save her.[27] In turn, the counter-theme is associated with the negative thoughts and situations involving him. So long as there is action the music disappears and is heard only to identify it with his thoughts, not with putting them into practice. For example, after arguing with Betsy or at the beginning of the disturbing scene in which a customer (Martin Scorsese himself) assures him, while he is being driven in the cab, that he will kill his wife. The explanation of how and why he will kill her comes during a musical silence... this is something that does not concern Travis and therefore the explanation has no need of the counter-theme being applied. In fact, by not using it, the taxi-driver's indifference is emphasized. But when the customer explains that he will kill her with a Magnum .44 something wakes up inside Travis: the idea that nothing more is needed than a gun to resolve the world's problems. It is then that the counter-theme again dominates the scene and his thoughts, and this continues when he is alone, during his soliloquy before the mirror. Another example comes in the scene in which Travis, wanting to remove Iris from her low life, manages to stay with her for breakfast. After making the date, we hear the Jekyll theme (Travis/Redeemer), but as he leaves the room he bumps into the caretaker and we hear the counter-theme (Travis/Avenger). The two contradict each other while at the same time—both being needed—they struggle for Travis' mind.

Let us skip to the final part of the film at the moment when Travis gets out of the taxi and kills the pimp. He goes toward the hostal and begins the massacre, all done in absolute musical silence. Travis does not think but acts and, as indicated earlier, the music is in his thoughts not in his actions. Finally, the massacre ends. As Travis lies agonizing and the police enter the room, the counter-theme reappears with force. Within it we hear a broken and sinister reference to the Jekyll theme. Has Hyde beaten Jekyll? Everything would indicate that this has happened. Not only has the counter-theme completely outdone the theme that was confronting it but furthermore expands victorious as the camera moves out of the hostal and away

---

[27] There is only one curious exception and that is when this theme is heard diegetically as the pimp attempts to convince Iris not to give up prostitution. He puts on a record and begins to dance to the theme. Although the music does not come from Travis' mind, he is thinking about Iris and his desire to save her. In this way, Travis and his cause both burst on to the scene. In addition, the fact that Travis' hopes are dashed by the pimp's dance turns out to be disheartening and pathetic.

from the street filled with police. This is the first ending. The film could end there and offer the result that Jekyll had been beaten by Hyde. The counter-theme in this case would come out as main theme of the soundtrack. However, the film has an ironical surprise and this is that Travis has survived and has now become something of a national hero. We see his room filled with press clippings praising him for having saved an adolescent girl while, in voice-over, we hear Iris' father reading the letter of thanks written to his daughter's saviour. Now we hear the positive theme (the Jekyll theme) and Travis is little less than a legend. He goes back to his taxi and, quite by chance, Betsy (who earlier rejected and now admires him) is his first fare. Now the Jekyll sounds in all its splendour when she gets out of the cab and he continues to drive along the street and the final credits begin. This is the second ending, absolutely opposed to the first. It is the positive theme which fills all the dramatic space and the conclusion, inevitably, is that the duel has been won by this theme, which logically would have to be the soundtrack's main theme. There is a third ending, but this does not come out of the literary script but develops entirely from the music. In the closing credits (and within the final theme) we hear the Jekyll theme (apparently the main theme), but suddenly, the drumrolls of the counter-theme break in and this theme reappears, hitting the spectator right to the very end of the film. This is the third ending: everything goes back to being as it was at the beginning. Nothing has changed. Hyde is not dead. Nor is Jekyll. The same duality. The very same conflict. There is no main theme, only two central themes that will have to continue struggling to dominate for ownership. Here we have a music script that keeps on developing from the beginning of the film to its very last second. The audience who, at the beginning of the final credits get up from their seats or turn off their television, miss it all. In this, his very last film, Herrmann gave the same importance to the initial and the final theme, making them absolutely equal.

- **Sub-theme**

A sub-theme is the submission of one theme to another and its insertion in the other theme, which, in principle, assumes a dominant position. If, for example, in a main theme (A) we incorporate a fragment of a central theme (B), this will remain subordinate to the main theme (Ab) and will turn into its sub-theme. There are three factors that would justify such use: a reference (spatial level of references); to underline the position of dominance; or to provide it with a larger field of operation. In any of these situations the use of a theme as a sub-theme must be understandable and therefore must arise from a central theme (or from a main motif which will be explained later) so that the spectator knows what is being referred to, subjected or amplified. Thus, the dominant theme may be a central theme but also a secondary theme, in this case limiting it to a provisional position. A secondary theme, devoid of any real significance, cannot become a sub-theme.

When two themes are linked together under equal conditions (A to B to form AB) there is no sub-theme, simply the union of two themes. On the other hand, the fact that A absorbs B and the result is not equal (Ab) implies that from the sub-theme (b) we are obtaining a specific narrative or dramatic value. In terms of reference, the obvious intention is to incorporate its significance on the screen. A young man may be thinking of his absent love, which is specified if, in the theme of the grief-stricken young man (A), we hear the theme of his beloved as a sub-theme (b). Here there is no situation of the power of one theme over another, but simply one of reference. In questions of control or power, what is being indicated at that moment is that, for some reason, there is no equality between what the two themes signify. The destruction of the central theme now converted into a sub-theme, for example. In this case, the sub-theme (b) remains completely subordinate to the dominant theme, which is exactly what happens to the *Jekyll* jazz theme in *Taxi Driver* (discussed above in the previous section) when it is heard as a sub-theme of the *Hyde* counter-theme in the first ending of the film. The two themes which had existed as equals now show that one has won over the other and has quite outdone it. Far from being merely a reference, it is total domination. The opposite can also happen with the sub-theme trying to occupy and dominate the space of the theme it displaces in a kind of harmful cancerous growth. In *District 9*, with music by Clinton Shorter, the central theme for Wickus, the suffering protagonist, incorporates at times the theme of general Fobus—the character it tries to subjugate and dominate as a sub-theme. Fobus is a personnage who tries to subjugate and dominate, thus creating a battle between the two in the music terrain. In *Up*, the theme for the sinister Charles Munz settles in as a sub-theme not only as a reference but as a warning of his danger. In *La vita è bella* where in the sequence where the death train is leaving, the love theme comes in as a sub-theme of the counter-theme which is completely subdued.

In the next section we shall examine motifs and fragments. Here, it will be possible to more fully develop the third option of the sub-theme explaining how it can function as such in order to make it more important.

- **Fragments and motifs: the leit-motif**

Music in films is not only made up of themes. There is also a place for fragments. These may be the sound of a flute, chords played on a guitar, tremolos on a piano or the dramatic effect of an orchestra. All are specific tools used to meet certain needs, such as to underline an impression or a sensation, to give more effect to a clap of thunder, ease a transition between sequences, etc. With barely a few notes and no further development it is possible to make an audience aware of the uneasy feeling a place or a character provokes, of a feeling of joy, or the calm of a landscape. There are three types—independent, developing and derivative fragments. Independent fragments are those that fulfil no other function than that of providing a specific musical impact at a determined moment, such as a dramatic orchestral effect. They do not add any narrative aspect to the music script but are simply bits of music put there to patch together specific moments.

Developing fragments begin as a fragment but which will go on gathering body until they attain the form of a musical theme. Derivative fragments, on the other hand, are those that arise from a musical theme that has been deconstructed and atomized to the point where it has been reduced to its most elemental expression. Developing fragments have a narrative use—showing growth whereas those derived may fit into a destruction or a reduction to basics of a music theme so that it remains present without having to be so completely. They can, of course, exist as such if they derive or arise from a theme. Or, if they have sufficient identity to be recognized and linked to the theme in which they develop so that they may be recognized as being motifs of that theme. These have body enough to be recognizable, along with their own personality and can be counted on to possess their own harmonic, melodic or rhythmic elements.

They are made up of only a few notes which, in spite of being brief, do provide some important indications, which is the reason why there cannot be an independent motif unless it is be a leit-motif, something we will discuss below.

Examples of derivative motifs are the indicators in code form already explained with regard to *Gladiator* and the film *How to Train Your Dragon*. In both cases, consisting of a few brief notes with their own identity, they will end up becoming part of a central theme. We very frequently find examples of derivative motifs when a central theme is reduced to the form of a motif either as a reference or an expression of its destruction, as in the case of *Taxi Driver*.

A leit-motif does not have to develop in the form of a theme in order to maintain its own identity but it can do so or a theme can be compressed and reduced to the form of a leit-motif. The leit-motif was introduced to films by Max Steiner and can be independent, developing or derivative. However, in this latter case it would stop being a motif and would convert into a theme. This is what happens with the John Williams theme for *Close Encounters of the Third Kind* which starts out as a communication reference and ends up as a grand symphonic musical theme that raises its category, its significance and its symbolism. The leit-motif relates to something specific and exclusive and by definition can neither be moved nor changed as it fulfils the function of music necessary to establish intellectual communication with the audience.

The film *King Kong* (Ernest B. Schoedsack, Merian C. Cooper, 1933) was one of the first to make use of a leit-motif: vibrant and intense notes applied to the figure of the gorilla, so that every time it was heard the music was making specific reference to King Kong, so that it was not always necessary to show the monster on the screen. With his leit-motif, King Kong was present although he could not be seen. As it is exclusive, when a leit-motif is applied to something it can only refer to the same thing from then on. If in King Kong, for example, it were used for something else, it would be confusing because all reference would be lost. It is not necessary to use it every time what it refers to appears on the screen, but it is necessary when the reference comes up, although not visually, that the motif be applied. That is to say, it is not because King Kong comes on the screen that the leit-motif should be heard but rather that, when the leit-motif sounds, King Kong appears on screen even though simply as a reference.

For decades the leit-motif was often used because of its usefulness in explaining things. Hanns Eisler justified its use in these words: *The ease with which they are recalled provides definitive clues for the listener, and they are also practical help to the composer in his task of composition under pressure. He can quote where he otherwise would have to invent.*[28] Chion also praised its usefulness: *The leit-motif gives the musical fabric a kind of elasticity, a smooth fluidity (...) If we reject its use to a greater or lesser extent it is not easy to find another rule of thumb.*[29] It may be used as often as is felt necessary or as many times as it serves the purpose for which it has been created.[30] One of the most famous cases is that of *Laura* (Otto Preminger, 1944) in which David Raksin's beautiful score was supported by the leit-motif for Laura with the aim of serving as a permanent reference, both romantic and somewhat enigmatic. This was used both both diegetically and incidentally some thirty times. Such abundant use was due to the many times the character is remembered or evoked by the other characters. Another film that pioneered the use of the leit-motif was *The Bride of Frankenstein* (James Whale, 1935) with music by Franz Waxman in which the composer expressed chaos with a combination of beauty and frenetic gloom, thus achieving a sensation of decadence and terror. He used four notes for Frankenstein's monster based on his grunting; three florid and exotic notes for the bride, which made possible the creation of an open melody that was used in a number of ways; and he gave Doctor Frankenstein a deliberately grotesque and crazy theme. With the combination of these three aspects in vanguard music Waxman created a landmark.

---

[28] Adorno, T. y Eisler, H.. «Composing for films» (Continuum, 2005) P 4

[29] "Le leitmotif assure au tissu musical una sorte d'elasticité, de fluidité glissante (...) Le jour ou onen a délaissé plus ou moins l'usage, il n'a pas été si facile de retrouver une autre règle du jeu". Chion, M.: Op. cit. P. 220

[30] Sometimes, indeed, it has been overdone. The terrifying leit-motif in Creature from the Black Lagoon (Jack Arnold, 1954) was eventually repeated 150 times.

As an exclusive and precise musical reference, the leit-motif has a use that must always be true. It cannot be used as a trick, given that once this has happened the spectator will no longer believe in it and the result would be confusion. If in *Jaws* the shark leit-motif (used impeccably here) had been introduced to confuse in the sequence of the false shark (when children playing with a plastic fin terrorized the bathers), from that moment on, one would be in doubt about its credibility. On the contrary, John Williams was honest in his use of the leit-motif. In the scene with the false shark there is not a note of music and nothing of leit-motifs.[31] Its big narrative advantage is the immediacy of its brevity. If *Jaws* depends on a leit-motif it is for practical reasons. It would not be viable to reference it with a theme that required a period of time the film just did not have. The shark moves rapidly and the music also had to be like lightning. This is more than reasonable but could the leit-motif be used outside the reference? In this case, the answer is no. At least, if it is still being used individually its use would warn of the presence of the shark but it would be difficult to generate any sensation other than fright. The most usual solution given to this problem is to insert a series of secondary themes, which makes it into a sub-theme to give it more substance, but without converting it into a theme. John Williams himself in *War Horse* (Steven Spielberg, 2011) linked, emotionally and intellectually, the young protagonist and his horse by an insistent motif used frequently in the first part of the film. On occasion this was developed as a theme, and then, in the long second part of the film it was not used at all, leaving the audience with a terrible feeling of emptiness, and was only picked up again in the epilogue, now as the main theme.

- **Progression of themes: repeated, varied and transformed**

When a theme is heard more than once during the music script it may be for aesthetic or narrative reasons. There are three ways a theme that is used more than once can progress—it can be repeated, varied or transformed. A repeated theme is that which sounds the same in different parts of the film; a varied theme is that to which

---

[31] A moment of tension was sacrificed for the benefit of the rest of the film. Furthermore, just as the sequence ends, the real shark bursts in, the leit-motif is heard and terror comes back into the film.

arrangements and/or variations have been added. Both keep their own meanings at all times and are therefore static themes in narrative terms. On the other hand, a transformed theme is that which, either by its repetition or its variation, changes its meaning slightly or substantially and may even come to mean the opposite of what it started out to be. It is the most practical way to transform the genetic code of a central theme and, because of this, a transformed theme is not static but dynamic. A secondary theme may be repeated or varied but only central themes have the ability to be transformed, although they, too, may be limited to repetition or variation.

The main theme of *The Third Man* (Carol Reed, 1949) by Anton Karas is repeated without transformation, in spite of changes in the story, but with these repetitions the music reaffirms a single impression, one that is static. In *Basic Instinct* (Paul Verhoeven, 1992), Jerry Goldsmith wrote a warm and sensual theme for the Sharon Stone character combining eroticism and mystery. As the impression to be transmitted was specific, the music was not transformed but simply repeated. Nor can we consider the main fanfare of the *Star Wars* saga as transformed music although we certainly can do so in the case of other central themes that change during the action. The Indiana Jones march John Williams wrote for *Raiders of the Lost Ark* (Steven Spielberg, 1981) was repeated all through the film without this altering its significance one iota. The James Bond theme by Monty Norman, in various films of the saga is heard in a great number of versions and variations without its significance changing in the slightest. There are other clear examples of music repeated and varied, which reaffirm a single fixed impression. On the other hand, many films, such as *Amarcord*, one of the most emblematic films of composer Nino Rota, show a solid fabric of transformed music. Here, the nostalgic and evocative tone of the main theme goes through various transformations, one of them particularly sad interpreted by a blind accordeon-player in one of the film's most beautiful moments.

Transformed music gives a boost to a theme, modulating and changing it. However, these changes must respond to a specific meaning showing, for instance, that the protagonist is depressed whereas before he was happy; and that this can be done through the music and not from what the literary script sets out can be extremely useful. Generally, these transformations come from variations, from musical themes that alter both their form and their significance (an optimistic melody that becomes pessimistic), although sometimes this can be achieved through repetition. A recent and quite brilliant example was the music by Harry Escott for the controversial independent film *Shame* (Steve McQueen, 2011). In this film, the protagonist is a heterosexual man who lives trapped in his sexual obsessions, which he attempts to satisfy without this causing him any apparent conflict. In one early sequence he is travelling in the subway and sees a young girl who returns his stare and smiles at him. He sees her as a possible sexual objective and during the sequence, we hear a musical theme (which will be the main theme) that expresses, in its genetic code and in a very balanced way, an impression of contained pathos (afflicted, suffering, in an adagio-type form), but which clearly expresses victory, power and triumph at the same time. This girl is going to be another of his many conquests although finally he decides against going after her when she gets out of the carriage. Much later, when he is caught up in a spiral of degradation and personal catharsis and has lost all feelings of security about himself, the same theme is repeated in another sequence. Almost desperate, he goes into a homosexual bar to try to find a way to ease his anxiety. In the process—from the moment he enters until he finds transitory relief—the identical music is repeated, although its significance is quite different... there is no sign of victory or power but only of pathos, even more afflicted and desperate.

How do we make a musical theme transform its meaning without changing its form? Quite simply, through the implication and the development of the context in which it is placed. It is obvious that to show this process of degradation taking place in *Shame*, it is of the utmost importance to have shown the previous scene, so that when it is used again it works through comparison and contrast. Had there not been a previous reference where it functioned, even partially, as a sign of power and dominion, the music would not have been able to express what was clearly intended, the protagonist's *fall to hell*. This is because the music ends up magnetizing and being magnetized by the sequence where it is applied, which makes it possible to emphasize one of its elements while making the others practically invisible. This is why, as was commented on earlier, the musical theme for *Vertigo* by Bernard Herrmann means something so different when it is applied in *The Artist*.

In all the first part of *La vita è bella* the two central themes Nicola Piovani wrote for the character of Guido (the one for his optimism and the one dealing with his love for his wife) change various times but always signify the same thing: *life is beautiful and I am crazily in love with you*. Nevertheless, in the second part where the counter-theme of horror, (merely indicated in the first part) reappears with force, these two themes are transformed, inevitably changing their significance. *Life is beautiful* becomes *We must survive all this* and *I am crazily in love with you* changes to *Where are you, my love?* In the epilogue, once the counter-theme has ended, these themes recover their original meaning when they are inherited by the surviving son.

In *Rosemary's Baby* an interesting effect is produced with the main theme. This theme, a cradle-song hummed by Mia Farrow, is presented as the initial theme where it is exactly that: a cradle song, although with a slightly sinister background. Later on, the theme turns into the concept of motherhood, or more specifically the desire for motherhood, and is heard again, now transformed, when Rosemary's pregnancy is confirmed over the telephone. Here, however, the theme is somewhat charged without malice, as when, after feeling very sick, she celebrates the fact that the baby is moving inside her—a moment that gives rise to a montage of sequences where we see how this affects her life at home. The music expressing the innocent and pure longing for motherhood is repeated in a dream in which she is holding the infant in her arms. All through the film and before we get to the final sequences, this theme has shared space with a series of musical forms, all of which, with the exception of a brief referential motif, are secondary themes intended to emphasize the threat of Evil which, by comparison, underline even more strongly the goodness represented by the theme of motherhood. However, when Rosemary flees from the house after she suspects they want to rob her new-born son, she goes to seek the help of her old gynaecologist and the theme is heard again when she is being driven home. Here it clearly is transformed and no longer signifies what it did before but expresses motherhood in danger and, furthermore, in a very disturbing way. In the final scene, once Rosemary accepts being the mother of the son of Satan, the theme becomes the final theme running with the credits. It is exactly the same theme heard as the initial theme (with regard to the one repeated) but its meaning is very different: where it earlier reflected motherhood, the film now ends signifying the acceptance of that motherhood. But it is not the same thing... not by a long shot.

Something similar takes place in *Signs*. As initial theme, the main theme expresses Evil with all its strength and power. This is referential music (of the extraterrestrials) which, in the film, takes up various invasive and hostile spaces, until its stupendous transformation in the final scene. Now the main motif of the theme expresses redemption, in a kind of religious conversion that coincides with what the literary script explains about the protagonist. As final theme (a variation of the initial theme), it no longer represents anything evil but rather rest and peace. In *Evil Dead* the exact opposite happens: Roque Baños' main theme unites the protagonists with a dramatic but hopeful spirit, but ends up being contaminated by the evil music and, as final theme, becomes a macabre dance which represents the triumph of Hell.

Anothers interesting examples of the movement of a theme during a music script is found in the sophisticated film *Inception* and in the dramatic *La migliore offerta* (*The Best Offer*. Giuseppe Tornatore, 2013). The main theme of *Inception* (the totem, a top which is used to know if one is having another dream or is in the real world) is presented in the initial theme in the form of a code and is developed throughout the film, broadening both its concept and its presence, until it ends up as the main theme linked to the protagonist Cobb, representing his feelings of blame. But at the end its significance changes from being the music of remorse to that of hope and, with this transformation, many of the protagonist's emotions have been explained. In *The Best Offer*, on the other hand, Ennio Morricone's romantic main theme begins by giving the protagonist hope but will become eventually infected (through the insertion of a musical fragment contained in the counter-theme) and will end up being absolutely devastating in a memorable finale.

Obviously, a musical theme may be repeated, varied and transformed, in turn and in whatever order is required. Whenever there is a transformation and its meaning has been modified, either slightly or substantially, it will need to be retransformed in order to recover its original meaning. This forms part of the structure of the music script. For obvious reasons, a theme that is to be transformed will need to involve the audience even more, so that they do not miss the reference and, even though it is not necessary that it be a main theme, it must, at least, be given priority over those themes that are not transformed. At times, this is so important in a music script that it demands there be no other music to interfere in the process. It needs a *clear territory* even if that involves sacrificing melodic moments for its sake. This is what happens in Maurice Jarre's soundtrack for *A Passage to India* (David Lean, 1984). The film starts off with an initial theme that is solemn and emphatic, emulating both the fascination for the exotic (India) and the power and pomposity of the British colonizers. This generic theme settles into a clever transition that takes it to the point where it becomes the expression of the mental and emotional (and sexual) turbulence of the protagonist so that it ends up expressing her instability. And there is no going back. In the rest of the film this music will refer only to her. In this specific case (and because of the risk involved) no other music could be allowed to interfere in the process, which explains why the score is so short.

This is the process throughout the evolution of the film. Over the credits we hear the initial theme which reappears when Adela, the protagonist, finds an abandoned temple with erotic statues. This scene supposes an inflexion both in the story and the music. Adela feels upsetting sensations, which will eventually bring about a national tragedy (because of her, India will rise up), which serves to reintroduce the theme now transformed with female voices and with the patina of fascination exchanged for a sensual tone, between erotic and lascivious, applied directly to Adela and thus losing its generic nature. From this moment on, each reappearance of the theme will make direct reference to her mental state. When Adela cannot get to sleep the theme is again transformed recalling the impact of her experience in the temple, indicating the excitement and instability of her mind. This music is so oriented to reflect her psychological evolution that anything other than diegetic music would distract the audience's attention and water down the theme's efficiency. At the moment when she undertakes the last stretch to reach the caves, the theme is applied again (only this time it is varied) underlining the relation between her being upset with her arrival at the place where the catharsis will come about. In this way, the music is taking the character to the drama's starting point. If the music had been inserted earlier, its dispersion would have altered the overall perception. It will be used again later on when Adela is called to declare in court. The insertion of a derivative fragment will show her mental confusion and make evident her fear of facing the truth. Had there been room for more music, it could have been added freely after the drama was resolved, as it would not have interfered then with the main theme's evolution. In most cases a transformed theme can share space with other music, even when this, too, has been transformed. It all depends on what is set out in the film's music script.

5.2. Film scores without a thematic structure

Film scores, whose discourse depends on the hierarchical differentiation of themes and on their being positioned in a logical order, respond to the film's narrative that, to a greater or lesser extent, needs music to cover it. There may be times, of course, when this is not applicable—when no themes in a score are more important than others and narrative additions are not desired. Yet this does not make the music less important.

In a number of the films by Woody Allen or Quentin Tarantino, music is absolutely part and parcel of the film. However, none of these scores is narrative but rather chromatic, related to the film's ambiance and, in any case, are used to resolve specific scenes and make them more understandable, more animated, more enjoyable or dramatic. But this is, and quite legitimately so, music whose overall narrative responsibilities are simply sequential. In the case of Woody Allen there is often a certain homogeneity in the type of music he applies in his films (be it jazz or classical), while Tarantino generally uses a greater range of music, he knows how to interweave it in the film so that it makes up something solid and is not disperse. There are films that do not need narrative music and directors who make use of it only when their films need it. Tarantino and Allen have not yet dispensed with narrative music but there are directors, such as Martin Scorsese and Francis Ford Coppola, who have alternated its use according to the film. There is a musical discourse in *The Age of Innocence* (1993) but not in *Godfellas* (1990); it appears in *The*

Godfather but not in *Tucker: the Man and His Dream* (1988), to cite a couple of examples from each of these directors. An unstructured score may respond to aesthetic aims, even when the decisions made are inadequate or slow down the flow of the film. Nevertheless, the mere fact that music is applied means that it responds to a specific need, however elementary this may be. Though it should always be remembered that, should a film need to be made clearer, the music itself cannot do this. Furthermore, composers often have to suffer the results of poor directorial decisions or factors imposed from outside.

In any case, there are times when a film needs to avoid the order provided by thematically structured music precisely because of that very order. It has to avoid this to be able to form its own narrative discourse—of disorder and confusion. *Planet of the Apes* is one of the most brilliant examples. It is impossible to determine which the main theme is or the central themes in Jerry Goldsmith's music because they just do not exist. All the music navigates in the same direction with great unity of style. This is atonal music, primary, rough, ancestral and archaic. It is music for a dehumanized place, hostile and claustrophobic (even in open spaces), with no reference of any kind that might help the audience find answers and explanations. Without recognizable references, the music contributes to chaos rather than order. From the beginning, different percussions—each with its own rhythm and in no particular order, generate the feeling of primitive sound to suggest the beginning of the Universe and of Life itself. Goldsmith develops the idea of an unknown and inhospitable land using harsh, savage music that transmits a sensation of anxiety and anguish in the face of the unknown. It is music of another world, overwhelming and oppressive, with only slight melodic references which pass almost unnoticed in this battery of ancestral musical elements. But one is able to hear the beginnings of melody, although from far away, as if some human reference might be there somewhere distant in space and time. Nevertheless, some humanizing factor emerges when they find the first sign of life—a plant, scarecrows, water and, finally, human beings. From this moment on, everything appears less abstract and the music suggests known elements that balance between the abstract, the archaic and a certain humanization, although this depends on what is happening to the protagonist.

5. Distribution of Music

One of the most interesting scenes is when the apes are hunting the humans where the references, such as hunting horns, bring to mind a familiar environment. This is a distressing scene where the percussion mixes with the hunting horns and guttural sounds that are disconcerting. The distinct elements evolve chaotically with independent rhythms to create a macabre ballet, both oppressive and anxiety-provoking, suggesting a gruesome dance of death. The composer's strategy has been to take a physical element of the film— the hunting horns (although these do not appear on the screen)—and introduce them as musical elements symbolizing persecution, the hunt and the death of living creatures, in this case, humans. It is therefore an example of integrated music where the mix of hunting elements with the idea of a dance of death creates a grotesque situation that generates a feeling of distress. Finally, the entire strategy of the film score culminates in the beach scene. In the first part of this scene, when the protagonist is fleeing with Nova, the percussions added to a few wind instruments contribute to complete the idea of an oppressive space. When the protagonist discovers that in reality this space was his own land, the music disappears because the mystery has disappeared. The land becomes familiar and known and now cannot be seen as aggressive. The only threat is to human existence itself which ends up condemned to disappear in silence. It is with this silence that the film begins and this is how it ends, going back to nothing, as if Humanity itself has been condemned to extinction, emptiness, silence and death. Jerry Goldsmith wrote an extraordinary and exemplary music script for the film, not needing any recourse to a thematic structure. This would have been greatly counter-productive, as the audience might well have searched for specific answers in each piece of music used and, not finding them, would have been left feeling even more vulnerable and abandoned.

A film like *The Artist* has no musical structure because it is made, as most films were in the Twenties when the music was interpreted live, in a continuous succession of themes for specific sequences. Musical discourse and the involvement of music in film narrative would take time to become consolidated over the years, although many silent films had structured film scores. In any case, the development of a structured musical discourse would end up being used in the majority of films because of its great usefulness. This was the only reason that other possible options were passed by, and not just for reasons of aesthetics or ambience. Today, avoiding order to promote disorder or simply not delegating narrative responsibility to the music is not seen as often, although it is still used.

There are music scripts that try to trick you into believing they are destructured in order to generate a sensation of disorder and chaos when, in fact, they are perfectly ordered. An excellent example of this is the British film *Notes On a Scandal* (Richard Eyre, 2006) with music by Philip Glass. Here, Judi Dench plays Barbara, a despotic and solitary old woman who lives alone with no friends or confidants and governs her high school students with an iron hand. Her world changes when she meets Sheba (Cate Blanchett), the new professor of art, with whom she becomes friends and secretly falls in love. When she discovers that Sheba has a relationship with a student, she takes advantage of the situation to begin a brutal and pitiless quest to get her to leave her husband and children and go to live with her. This is a bitter film with two protagonists linked by a secret. The blackmail that Sheba suffers becomes more and more suffocating and Barbara's power over her increasingly morbid and destructive. Philip Glass wrote an obsessive and repetitive music score that played with pieces diabolically similar—while at the same time different in their detail and expression, with no recognizable central themes—which turn around themselves and at the end of the film return to the same point of departure. This sensation of obsession, apparently repeated time and time again, homogenizes the score, making it chaotic and unpredictable. Almost everything is dedicated to emphasizing Barbara's changing emotions while giving her considerable strength, which is precisely what she physically lacks. The music even reaches places where its "owner" is not present but still causing the same damage.[32] Every manifestation of the music is the result of an expressive function, be it her coldness, her being in love, her anger, her visceral hatred, her contempt. There is a main theme but it goes through so many transformations that it seems not to exist other than as a reference, and the music deals more with destruction (which the

---

[32] In one scene, Sheba tries to maintain an ordinary conversation with her husband while also attending to the sentimental problems of her adolescent daughter. At both moments, however, in her own home, we hear Barbara's invasive music which blocks out the audience's interest in either of the two conversations and reveals the dangerous power Barbara is beginning to wield over Sheba.

character provokes) than with construction (the relationship with the other character). The final scene is extremely interesting when, after the whirlwind, everything begins again with a new victim and the same indifference of the she-wolf toward her. In this process the music has passed through various dramatic levels: delight (the excitement and illusion as well as knowing she has power over Sheba's destiny); coldness (Barbara calculates the steps to be taken in order to catch Sheba); fury (she goes crazy because the victim does not respond to what she has hoped for); and even weakness (Barbara begins to see herself as a loser). Except for the music in diegesis and some incidental themes, all the music focusses on the incessant threat from Barbara. Even though the literary script makes it seem she is quite in control of her actions, the music script contradicts this and exposes not only her enormous evil but her absolute lack of restraint, both emotional and psychological. So much so that, when Sheba finally manages to unmask Barbara (when she finds her diary), the music which up to that point has been the music of her power, now abandons her, turning against her. Barbara is shown at last as an extremely weak creature.[33] All of this gives a lasting impression of chaos and lack of planning in a film score that, on the other hand, is perfectly structured.

5.3. Songs

The use of songs usually is the result of commercial considerations but also may be used with aesthetic and dramatic intention and even, though not as much, for narrative purposes. We are referring here to songs in films that are not musicals that feed off those and are never questioned. They may be criticized if they are of doubtful quality but the spectator does not question their being used.

Among film scores there are those that, while not belonging to the musical film genre, have songs incidentally applied, which are

---

[33] This weakness will not last long. Shortly after, in a wonderful montage of parallel scenes, Barbara begins to write a new diary while Sheba goes home with her husband. Both scenes are linked by the same music… optimistic for Barbara and clearly dramatic for Sheba and later on comes the ending (which we have already discussed) where everything goes back to the starting point. Barbara will continue on, a she-wolf in search of prey with Sheba as one of her victims with wounds still to be healed.

exquisite and are used correctly with notable results. In some cases these are already existing songs while others are original or a combination of both. Tom Waits, for example, was the author of a magnificent film score of songs for *One from the Heart* (Francis Ford Coppola, 1982), very well integrated in the context of both story and ambience. In *Pulp Fiction*, the already existing songs are also perfectly integrated, as is the case in *The Commitments* (Alan Parker, 1991), *Good Night, and Good Luck* (George Clooney, 2005), *Juno* (Jason Reitman 2007). *Malcolm X* (Spike Lee, 1992) and *The Aviator* (Martin Scorsese, 2004). In these last two films, they were combined with original music by Terence Blanchard and Howard Shore respectively where the music deals with the dramatic, while the songs create ambience—a fairly common division of responsibilities when this double use is involved.

Unfortunately, the use of songs in film has, for some time now, been greatly abused, taking up space where they do not belong, either in narrative or dramatic terms and, what is even worse, taking space away from original music. These are largely there for commercial reasons—to sell the soundtrack or to promote the film itself. They do considerable damage to the composer's narrative work and only serve to exchange artistic intentions for commercial purposes. We can see this in the almost systematic *robbery* carried out in the final credits in films where instead of the final theme that should conclude the dramatic and narrative outcome of the music script, they insert a song (or several) that have nothing to do, not even aesthetically, with what has been heard all through the film.

It is quite different if the songs are integrated with what has been developed throughout the music script and form an inseparable part of the narrative discourse. A song reaches the spectator very directly, even more than an instrumental theme, given that the spectator is always aware of its presence and can more easily retain its melody, which prepares the way for its successive instrumental applications, especially if it is to function as a central or main theme. Dimitri Tiomkin did this marvelously well with the song *Do Not Forsake Me Oh My Darling*, with which *High Noon* (Fred Zinnemann, 1952) opened and closed. This beautiful, sad ballad served as a melodic reference for much more dramatic use in the music script when, in an instrumental version, it was used to underline the protagonist's anguish. Furthermore, it was a song that had huge commercial success and opened the door to other songs used in a similar way, both by Tiomkin and others such as Henry Mancini, a composer who made much use of songs as a platform for submerging the spectator in the musical discourse of his films: *Breakfast at Tiffany's* (Blake Edwards, 1961), *Days of Wine and Roses* (Blake Edwards, 1962) or *Two For the Road* (Stanley Donen, 1967), whose main themes were presented in the form of a song and later developed instrumentally. Michel Legrand and Marvin Hamlisch did the same thing, as well as so many others who knew how to integrate songs into the essence of their music. The Sixties and Seventies were very fruitful in this way of using songs and right up to the present time this has been the case, although not always linking a song to the rest of the instrumental music but sometimes using it to mark the end of a section. In the British film *Alfie* (Lewis Gilbert, 1966) a curious thing happened. The jazz music was by Sonny Rollins but for U.S. distribution a song by Burt Bacharach (titled the same as the film) was added at the end. Furthermore, it was a song that described the protagonist very well. Other songs that worked well as final resumés were *One More Hour* by Randy Newman for *Ragtime* and *Burn it Blue* by Elliot Goldenthal for *Frida*.

The first shot where a song is applied in a film helps to narrate through the words—which bring text from the literary script to the music script—important aspects of the film and its characters. This was done admirably in *Magnolia* with the song *Save Me* with which it covered many of the characters. In much the same way, *Vois sur ton chemin* by Bruno Coulais was used in the film *Les choristes*.

It is obvious that songs can form part of the musical structure of a film score and take on the elements and characteristics explained above with regard to the music (whether original or existing, incidental or diegetic, integrated, empathetic, or as main theme, central theme, etc.). While they are not necessarily obstacles to the musical discourse they should not be used to detract from it.

6. The Music Script

The elements discussed in the previous chapters make up what is necessary to construct a well-ordered and logical music script that meets the needs of a film, facilitates its comprehension and is able to transmit emotion and information.

It should be understood that a film narrates a segment of the life of one or more characters and that there has been a "before" and an "after" to the story that is not explained. At times, some aspects of the past or the future are related in the film either in flash-back or flash-forward, or are perhaps explained by the characters in the literary script. Unless, of course, the starting point were to be the very beginning of the Universe or that the film should end with the annihilation of the Universe itself. However, if the protagonist of the film is 40 years old, the previous 39 years and all his years still to come will only be told as they come up within the particular fragment of his life dealt with in the film. And this will be so for all the characters who appear in the film.

This is always the case in a film's literary script but only now and then does it happen in the music script. The narrative discourse of the music script starts out from zero where there is no musical past, and it ends when the segment of life (determined as the film's story) ends. There is no musical future—the music covers whatever it must from the first scene (or initial credits) to the final scene (or closing credits). The composer must make a coherent whole from what is merely a fragment of the life of one or more characters, unless, of course, this past or future forms part of the film. In that case, the music will move into those spaces of time, as happens in *C'era una volta il West* where the starting point of the music shared by Frank and Harmonica is a past event explained in flash-backs. However, this will not happen if the music is not applied at a spatial level of references, where those references make mention of aspects of the past or future that the spectator understands. It goes without saying that this is also the case if, at the end of the film, the composer returns cyclically to the initial point of departure, as happens in *Taxi Driver* or in *Notes on a Scandal*. Nevertheless, if in a first sequence, we see a man coming out of jail the spectator now knows that this character has a past which will or will not be explained in the fragment of his life chosen as the story of the film. But the music itself does not have a past. And if, at the end of the film, the protagonists should get married and we know that their lives will continue on, the music—although it may well give some broad indication of what their future life might be—will not go beyond the space of the film,

Because of all this, the composer must convert a fragment of a life into something approximating a complete life which begins and ends with the film. The first essential step in achieving this is to know all about that fragment of life dealt with in the film—what it is telling us, what aspects it focusses on and those it deals with in passing. In deciding whether or not to consider the past and the future (that is not narrated), it is important to understand and accept that the music should centre on what must be emphasized and developed rather than aspects of lesser importance. Trying to cover absolutely everything will lead to ending up with a confused and overdone result. The very first consideration is the amount of music that is going to be needed.

6.1. How much music?

"Nothing annoys more than music that is used so often that when it is really needed the audience no longer hears it"[34]

John Morris

That was how Morris justified the scarcity of music in *The Elephant Man* and it also explains the short length of his film score for *Young Frankenstein*. Both, however, are impeccable examples of good film music. On the other hand, Morris had written an extensive, varied and detailed score for *Silent Movie* (Mel Brooks, 1976), which, it must be said, is an exemplary creation. What then is it that determines how long a film score should be? The best answer is also the most obvious: as long as the film needs it to be. In the broad spectrum that goes from not applying a single note to filling the film

---

[34] LP «The Elephant Man» (Pacific Arts, PAC 8.143, 1980).

with music, the only thing that truly matters is that the music has a reason to be there. It must be fully justified.[35] Some films need very little music or none at all, while others can only be constructed if accompanied by a great deal of music. One reason for this is the predominance of dialogue. Although at times it is useful to include music with the dialogue, music and dialogue together can be uncomfortable bed partners and interfere with each other. What is more, in films like *A Woman Under the Influence* (John Cassavetes, 1974) or *Interiors* (Woody Allen, 1978), the silences are as important as the words and music could well interfere with those silences. On the other hand, films by Federico Fellini, Akira Kurosawa or Luchino Visconti are very visual and, while the word is important, the picture is even more so. Their splendid settings and dress contribute to a spectacle in which music helps enormously. This is not saying that directors like Buñuel, Bergman, Cassavetes have not used music from time to time, because they certainly have done so, although largely it has been existing music. *Viridiana* (Luis Buñuel, 1959), for example, accompanies some of its best sequences with music, and Ingmar Bergman's, *Viskningar och rop* (Cries and Whispers, 1973), makes a particularly superb use of music.[36]

There is nothing worse than unnecessary music and every good composer must know how to restrain him/herself because, in principle, it would be preferable that a scene be without music than that the music applied be unnecessary. The brilliant composer stated:

---

[35] If it is incidental music because, as we have already seen, diegetic music justifies itself.

[36] This film tells the story of two sisters unhappily married who take care of another sister who is ill. There is no original music, but pieces by Mozart and Bach applied diegetically. The attention given the sick sister by the other two means that there is practically no conversation between them other than routine words exchanged. When the sick sister dies, one goes up to the other and begs that the relationship between them be again as it was when they were children, that the lack of communication end so that they might hug and kiss and tell each other things. She asks this insistently but the rejection is just as persistent on the part of her sister. And this is maintained until the reticent sister breaks down and hugs the other tightly. They begin to embrace and kiss each other, talking of things they have kept quiet about for years... but precisely at this moment we do not hear what they are saying! Instead, we hear music. It really does not matter what they are saying... they are saying it and that is what is beautiful. Neither is it important what music takes the place of their words. Thus, in this beautiful film there is only one scene with incidental music, but it is all that is needed.

"There's no need to put music in a picture unless you have some reason to say something or you feel the need for underlining or emphasizing, de-emphasizing or weighing (...) or doing what the film is failing to do, or can't do on its own".[37] At times, of course, it is impossible to do this, almost always because of outside pressure. Many Hollywood films from the Forties provide good examples, as composer Hugo Friedhofer once said: *"All the big studios had big orchestras under contract. And they had to utilize them. So the composer was forced to write more expansively and extensively than he might have liked".*[38] An excess of music when it is not necessary prejudices what is really required through saturation or even by the confusion it may cause, exactly the same way an excessively short score, for a film that needs much more music, will not satisfy the needs of the film and will make it less explanatory. There are plenty of examples. *Patton* (Franklin J. Schaffner, 1970) with music by Jerry Goldsmith has very little music (only a little more than 30 minutes for a film lasting more than three hours), but what is used is perfectly justified. At the other extreme, the long saga that began with *The Lord of the Rings: The Fellowship of the Ring* has abundant and sufficient music by Howard Shore. One must examine what the film needs if we want to know if it requires more or less music or if we are to judge whether the music has been excessive or scarce. Perhaps the best answer to the question *How much music does a film need?* would be *The less, the better*. Of course, *the less* may take up 80% or more of the film's total space.

6.2. What kind of music?

It is essential to settle on the style or styles of music necessary to define a film aesthetically and dramatically. The cinema has accepted all styles from the traditional to the most experimental, even a fusion of styles and the co-existence of various styles in the same film. While there has been much tolerance about the types of music used in film, the truth is that some styles have their limits. In fact, the history of music in the cinema has been a selective process in which

---

[37] Karlin,F,: «Listen to the Movies» (Schirmer Books, 1994). P.11.

[38] Ibid, P,75. This policy of the big Hollywood studios was a real torment for many composers who were obliged to produce long scores.

the only condition applied has always been how it meets the needs of the film. Starting out from this premise, the decision on style or styles may be conditioned or not: conditioned when the option is taken on the basis of geographical, historical or story factors; voluntary if the reasons have nothing to do with such criteria. For instance, if a film takes place in the 18th century the music chosen could be Baroque if one wants the score to carry the ambience of the period. However, the use of Baroque music is not obligatory *per se*. In many cases, contemporary music has been used in historical films.

The first conditioning criteria are geographical or related to location. The music comes from the place where the action takes place. *Alexis Zorba* (*Zorba the Greek*. Michael Caccoyannis, 1964), with a score by Mikis Theodorakis, quite logically uses Greek music because the film action takes place in Greece. The same reasoning comes up with Indian music by Ravi Shankar in *Gandhi* and Mychael Danna in *Life of Pi*, or with Mexican music in *Frida*, with a score by Elliot Goldenthal. Geographical and ethnic criteria for music are, in general, key determinants, although they make no sense if used out of context. And, in any case, the geographical/location criteria can certainly not be considered exclusive. This type of music may well be compatible with other styles, especially if one wants to transcend a purely local scene. It may be decided to forget the geographical factor and not use music related to locality at all. Japanese music is not necessarily needed simply because the action takes place in Japan. This is when the choice of style is not conditioned.

Something similar happens with the second conditioning criteria: the historical. Here the aim is to give the film music suitable to the period when the action takes place. A mediaeval film would have mediaeval music and one set in the crazy Twenties could make use of fox-trots, jazz, etc. Nevertheless, if there are no precise factors for giving a film music of the period, or if such a period did not exist as it is purely fictional, then the cinema is open to invention. Think back to the musical inventions in *Ben-Hur* with music by Miklós Rózsa, *Planet of the Apes* with a score by Jerry Goldsmith or *Blade Runner* (Ridley Scott, 1982) whose score is by Vangelis. In these cases, the composer clearly decided he would write music the audience could identify as being of the period narrated by the film. This is easiest to do in futuristic films given that there are no references, but in cases where such references do exist, even minimally, it is also valid if it helps to place the action. However, historical precision is not essential, quite the contrary, as it may be an impediment in the texture of certain scores, particularly because of the difficulties it might present in terms of expression or emotion. Anachronism is not a serious matter when one is conscious of playing tricks with *unreality* in order to present a fictitious reality. The score of *Il vangelo seccondo Matteo* (*The Gospel According to St. Matthew*. Pier Paolo Pasolini, 1966) is absolutely and bare-facedly anachronic. It is supported by original music by Luis Bacalov along with music by Bach. What was the predominant criteria here... historical or religious accuracy? To have favoured historical considerations, we would have a film score correct for its time but without the dramatic and evocative power that was achieved with the music by Bach, written a number of centuries after the time of Christ and based on the very Gospel itself.

The same thing happened in the version of *Romeo and Juliet* directed by Franco Zeffirelli. Nino Rota constructed a powerful score in which he used instrumentation of the period but applied in contemporary melodies. This made it possible to draw in a young contemporary public without making concessions to commercial considerations. Or in *Braveheart*, in which historical references in James Horner's music were merely the point of departure for constructing a Twentieth century score. If Rota or Horner had opted for historical accuracy in their music the films would never have had the same acceptance.[39] It is also possible to completely by-pass historical considerations and not include music of the period. In other words, just because a film takes place in the Sixties does not mean we have to hear Sixties' music. This is when the criteria of choice is not conditioned. In *Chariots of Fire* (Hugh Hudson, 1981), a film that takes place in the Twenties, there is no music of the period. Vangelis worked with electronic music.

The third conditioning factor is the narrative, which goes far beyond the geographical or the historical—although these two factors are naturally related to the story—and refers to when one or more of

---

[39] It is a matter of priorities. What is of most interest...the historical context or the essence of the story? Many period films, in fact, have universal themes so that the music may dispense with such criteria.

the characters in the film have some connection to a musical style, as would happen, for example, if they were musicians or liked to listen to a particular music. Jazz is used in *The Man with the Golden Arm* because the protagonist plays that music; the *Concierto for Mandolin* by Vivaldi constitutes the main part of the score of *La mariée était en noir* because the protagonist is listening to it.

When music, not conditioned by the above-mentioned factors (geography, history, etc.) is applied, the possibilities are endless. Nevertheless, some styles present more cinematic limitations than others. However, first of all, it is necessary to discuss melody, something practically banished from contemporary music but still used in film. This is not the place to explain why it is considered out-of-date or worn out in current composition, but it is necessary to show why film still needs it. Its importance has been such that back in the Forties the composer Hanns Eisler complained that *"more than anything else the demand for melody at any cost and on every occasion has throttled the development of motion-pictures"*.[40] Eisler was referring to something of stagnation in modes and forms but, in fact, film has been very tolerant of modes or forms that are not necessarily melodic and these have also worked wonderfully well. We should certainly keep in mind the relative inevitability of melody. There are many more musical styles that take advantage of melody than those that rule it out. Furthermore, it is an emotional arm of high calibre. In a melody it is easier to condense the basic elements of a character or concept and be able to transmit them more efficiently to the audience, by making them understandable and easier to accept. Another factor that has justified melody's frequent appearance in film, apart from the artistic, is commercial. On this point we may paraphrase Eisler's comment and state that *"commercial demands at whatever price and on whatever occasion have, more than anything else, throttled the development of music in film"*. Naturally, this does not, nor should it, mean that commercial considerations need be at odds with quality or that commercial music cannot be of maximum *usefulness* when applied to film. As, fortunately, the cinema accepts everything, even non-melodic music has found its own place to develop in film, alone or in combination with melodic music.

---

[40] Adorno, T, y Eisler, H. Op. Cit P. 8-9

Symphonic music is kingpin in cinema. This is so, as much for its being the form most used, as for its diversity. It can be used in drama as well as in action films, or those of terror, in Westerns, historical or romantic films... it fits into any genre. Symphonic music—although we should be more precise and say all types of symphonic music—dress up the spectacular, heighten the emotions, add solemnity to the visual and, most importantly, easily reach an audience. The entire history of sound film has gone from the classical symphonic music of Korngold and Prokofiev to the most contemporary music of James Newton Howard and Hans Zimmer. The forms perhaps have changed but the intentions are still the same or at least similar. On countless occasions, scores with orchestral power have benefitted the films in which they have been used. They can make images that set out to be grand even more grand, stronger or more intense while emphasizing specific emotions of the characters or situations dealt with in a sequence. Their field of involvement is so broad that their use in film has become static, showing very little evolution, at least in comparison with other styles. They may have changed forms but their intentions have already been exploited. Symphonic music is certainly not the highest level a piece of music can attain. It is not better just because it is symphonic, neither in musical nor in film terms. In fact, some film directors (and even composers) hide behind such music to make their limitations as creators less evident.[41] But, without a doubt, symphonic music has been, is and will continue to be a useful tool although it goes without saying that, depending on the circumstances, many other styles also work very well. For example, jazz certainly has evolved in its intentional application throughout the history of film; while pop, rock, electronic music, new age, experimental and many others have, at various times, proved their usefulness to film. What is important is to find the type of music adequate for the situations and characters so that it works well for the film.

---

[41] There is a tendency to give preference to symphonic film music that ends up being excessive. It is true that this is conditioned by commercial criteria, so that symphonic music has ended up becoming commercial. But it is no less so that these limitations are more evident in small groups (chamber orchestras, quartets, etc.) given that a considerable number of defects have been hidden behind the overwhelming sound of an orchestra of 70 or 80 musicians.

6.3. For what purpose and for whom?

It is not a good idea to overdo music in a film if this is not necessary. Often *less is more* and excessive music may reduce its dramatic effect or its power to communicate. In a film with a number of characters living through many different situations, the composer and the director should be aware that not all characters or situations, however relevant, can be defined in terms of music. One must choose what will go in and what must be left out, especially with regard to central themes, by reducing the music to the most essential or not putting in music at all. Unless it is a film with only a few characters the over-saturation of central themes will inevitably asphyxiate. A particularly fine example of a music script where characters are left without music is *Taxi Driver,* where the theme/counter-theme struggle of Jekyll/Hyde completely marginalizes any musical consideration for the other characters. Also in *Passage to India*, where the decision to put the music in the restless brain of the protagonist meant leaving some tempting scenes without any music at all. The same thing happens in *Atonement* where there is a love story about a couple who, in the first part of the film, have no music at all. All the space is taken up by the music of the girl who causes their tragedy. So much so, that it is only later when they have left her that they are able to enjoy music of their own. The more selective the attribution of central themes, the easier it will be to construct the film's musical script.

Whenever a director asks a composer to write "romantic" or "dramatic" music he is not really giving him/her a useful note. Nor (despite what he might think) is he being very precise if he asks for "happy-romantic" or "tragic-dramatic" if, with these indications he thinks he has explained everything he will need. There are hundreds of pieces of music that might be classed *romantic* or *dramatic*, all of them very different from each other. And while *happy* or *tragic* might reduce the field somewhat, it still leaves dozens of possible options. This usually means that a director has to ask again and again that a specific theme be rewritten until the composer hits on the specific type of music the director has in mind. When this happens, it is not usually because of the composer's lack of talent but because of the inadequate manner in which the director has explained it all. He might know what he wants but does not know how to communicate this to the composer.

Because of this, it is better that the director not talk about music at all but instead about the music's genetic code. Genetic codes—the break-down of the elements that make up the DNA of a musical theme, have been discussed earlier, but it is worth repeating again what we said before. A romantic theme, for example, might include such elements as optimism, innocence, intensity, happiness, the desire to live, a touch of immaturity and even simplicity... and the result would be a youthful love theme. In another romantic theme we could include goodness, calm, a modest touch of melancholy and a measure of dignity and we would have a theme suitable for two mature or elderly persons who love each other. The initial theme then has a genetic code made up of seven elements (optimism, innocence, intensity, joy, enthusiasm, immaturity and simplicity) while the second theme has four elements (goodness, calm, melancholy and dignity). Not all the elements making up the genetic code need be in the same proportion, given that a musical theme understood in this way is like a cocktail with different ingredients, each of them present in the exact dose necessary. When applied to whatever might be the object of interest (a scene or a character) these ingredients show what the object is made of and transmit this to the spectator in the form of clear information. Surely it would be more advantagous for the director, instead of simply asking the composer for a cocktail, to tell him what he wants in it.

The more detailed the genetic code of a musical theme, the easier it will be for a composer to turn it into music. If the director is not able to establish a list of those elements needed, then perhaps the composer may propose one. Come what may, these codes (especially in the audiovisual medium), need to be well established or the music will not end up being very solid, but full of hot air. It is not the same thing to write music for a beautiful landscape when your object is simply to make it more beautiful, as it is to write music that can explain something about a character. For this reason, when the music hopes to explain things, it must be integrated and if it is integrated it must have established a genetic code whose elements will together explain that character. Each of these elements—and it is important to stress this—will end up being highlighted when they are applied and the information and emotion they carry are transmitted to the spectator.

Depending on how these elements are combined and their importance in the theme, they will provide specific results. In the mature love theme, for example, (where the components are goodness, calm, a moderate touch of melancholy and a certain dignity), the focus might be more on goodness if a larger proportion is given to this ingredient in the cocktail. The remaining elements would still be there, although of secondary importance. As a result we would have a theme that, more than anything else, would deal with the good nature of the protagonists who long to be calm and maintain their integrity. If melancholy is what is given priority, we would be dealing with a pair of lovers conditioned by some affliction, but with the emphasis on their good nature, etc. All of these factors mean that asking a composer to write "romantic" or even "happy-romantic" music would be as useless as not having asked him for anything specific.

At the beginning of this book we discussed chess and the need to move the pieces adequately. This we might apply not only to writing a music script but also to the creation of a musical theme, where the 'pieces' are the various elements that make up the genetic code. A musical theme that combines, for example, sadness and hope in similar proportions will usually produce very interesting results. The element of melancholy means that, in some way or other, the music moves backwards while the optimistic element helps move the theme forwards, making it progress. This combination inevitably generates an expectation which helps the audience feel a dependence on the music as they will be waiting for the musical and emotional resolution that has to come. This apparent contradiction between the movement backwards and forwards at the same time, avoids allowing the audience to settle easily into the music to wait for some kind of resolution that will free them from the moderate discomfort generated by the melancholy. Pain (controlled) + Hope (in more open fashion) make up a good mathematical formula. With it, a character's feelings can be explained quite clearly. For this reason, it would be more practical to pose the task to the composer (or for the composer to suggest it to the director) in this way, than to simply talk about a "romantic theme". Furthermore, where themes with well determined genetic codes exist, we have only to alter the proportions allotted each element in order to achieve a complete transformation, and not simply a variation, so that it be perfectly understood. If, for example, we were to increase the feelings of pain and reduce the idea of hope, it would be a good indication of the theme's evolution and what it means.

Many people would consider Dimitri Tiomkin's beautiful main theme for *The Fall of the Roman Empire* as romantic but, if we take note of its genetic code, its DNA, it is much more than this. Tiomkin presented it as an initial theme and in it we find the dramatic essence of the entire film. It is a simple and romantic theme which grows in intensity, embellished by two quite different instruments: a powerful organ and a delicate zither. In essence, this theme expresses two elements. First and most notably, a tone of controlled sadness that evokes the love of the two protagonists condemned to a fateful end by a hostile environment; and secondly, although to a lesser extent, the solemnity of a specific historical period that emphasizes the idea of an empire that is collapsing. There is bitterness but also hope in the romantic part of the film whereas, in the other part, all is dark and pessimistic. Within this contradiction love ends up winning out in the end, which greatly reinforces its significance and also moves along what has to happen in the film. This is something that can be achieved when the theme has a well determined and proportioned genetic code. Something similar is found in Alfred Newman's lovely main theme for *The Diary of Anne Frank* (George Stevens, 1959), which underlines the innocence of the protagonist and the simplicity of her personality in contrast to the cruelty of the world in which she is forced to live. However, this is not really a theme applied to reflect her present-day situation but is aimed more at evoking her happy past, hope for the future and, more than anything else, the enormous dignity of the girl herself and of the whole Frank family. This theme thus comes out of the sum of innocent love + dignity + pain and the result is perfect. In the no less wonderful main theme by Georges Delerue for *Agnes of God* (Norman Jewison, 1985) we see the sum of spirituality + inner peace + affliction + hope with the result that the music, which is always moving forward, presents the best possible ending for this film about redemption. Also convincing, and especially interesting, because it goes through a major evolution from its start as an initial theme until it ends as the final theme, is Elmer Bernstein's theme for *Far from Heaven* (Todd Haynes, 2002). This romantic melody is not so much about the love between two people (although it is that, too), as about the love of oneself, given that the protagonist is a long-suffering woman of the Fifties, whose ideal world comes crashing down when she discovers the infidelity of her husband and falls in love with a black man. The music brings together the concepts of the pain of pure love and the need for liberation and offers as a result music that covers the woman with great dignity. For *To Kill a Mockingbird* (Alan J. Pakula, 1962) Bernstein had written another theme well defined in its genetic code. Presented as an initial theme—which included the concepts of goodness, childish innocence, hope and fragility—and this is how the film began, its dramatic features already set out in this musical theme.

If it is a matter of putting music to a character, working out the genetic code of the personage is extraordinarily important and the same is true for concepts. Whether you are a composer or director, this is a good moment to think what might be the genetic codes of music for Don Quixote de la Mancha, Hamlet, Napoleon Bonaparte, Joan of Arc, Winston Churchill, Marie Curie, Abraham Lincoln, Emiliano Zapata, Gandhi and others. In some of these you could include ethnic factors in the genetic codes (Hispanic, French, Mexican music...) while in others this would not make much sense. You may be able to explain these codes by including aspects which, while generic, make them unique. You would not give the same stubbornness to Don Quixote as to Napoleon nor would the same perseverance apply equally to Marie Curie and to Gandhi, because these factors combine with others and offer a particular result. Those you decide on are what will define them. And what works for these literary and historical personages, works in the exact same way for the characters in the literary script of a film, as well as for concepts such as war, victory, defeat, triumph, failure. Give them their own DNA and you will make each of them unique. For this reason, however, it is imperative that one be selective so as not to cause confusion. This means there should not be too many characters or concepts blessed with this kind of musical support.

In *Lo imposible* (*The Impossible*. J.A. Bayona, 2012), a film relating the events suffered by a family following the tsunami that devastated the coasts of South-East Asia in 2004, the main theme by Fernando Velázquez does not deal with the characters, nor even with their sentiments. It is music for a concept—union moving toward reunion. Naturally, this concept involves sentiments. However, it is not a theme of love, nor of anguish, although these emotions end up forming part of its genetic code. This process begins in the opening moments of the film by way of a clever symbolic and metaphoric manoeuver: the clients of a hotel dine calmly one night and after dinner let loose a series of flying lamps into the air. The scene is harmonious and peaceful and it is at this moment when we hear, for the first time, the musical theme that will be the film's main theme. It is a melody that covers all of those present. Nevertheless, one of the children of the protagonist family warns that the lamp they let loose is off-course and has separated from the others. And this is exactly what will happen to them… and what is going to happen also to the music, which, after that calm night, will no longer belong to everyone but will be centered on the family, and will therefore, be shared. After this point of departure, the main theme takes on a long narrative and emotional course. In order not to put anything in its way, the music for the ambience and the devastation is reduced to a minimum and is resolved with various secondary themes with no other pretension than to simply resolve sequences. However, none of these secondary themes contains any other narrative code, but is simply emotional. The course of the main theme is thus completely clear.

Let us see what happens in two animation films to which we have already referred—*Up* and *How to Train Your Dragon*. Both films have a great deal of music, all of it solidly constructed and ordered so that the discourses of the respective music scripts are clear and transparent. At its dramatic levels the music of *Up* offers a sense of adventure, love, innocence and menace. Among all of its musical themes three are central, one of which is the main theme. In addition, there are numerous secondary themes.

The main theme--the key emotional and narrative piece of the story—is a magical waltz that brings joy, emotion, nostalgia, sadness and courage and which as a result changes considerably, being intimate and also expansive. It appears on more than ten occasions and never sounds the same, nor means exactly the same thing. At first, it comes in as a derivative fragment to then become a theme expressing the love between Carl and his beloved Ellie. It is especially emotional in the beautiful montage of sequences that narrates their life in common, until she dies, where it takes on a number of nuances (love, happiness and also pain). From then on, every time he thinks of her, when he sees the house they built together, when he looks through her things, when he goes through her photo album, this waltz will be heard to personify his beloved at the spatial level of references. However, it also changes to become the music of adventure, of the desire to fulfill their dream of taking the house to Paradise Falls. From the moment the house begins to fly over the city, the music sounds magnificent and expansive. After that, the theme will continue to change either as a melancholy reference to his wife and a sign that the adventure is in danger, or as evidence that the strength to go on has been renewed. Finally, in the last scene, Carl shares this theme with little Russell as a generous and emotional gift, even though the child has his own central theme, (the music of innocence, childhood, curiosity and dreams), which seems very simple when compared with the main theme, but is only apparently so. It appears and disappears with the boy, varying at times but never transforming. In its early appearances, the theme has an amusingly invasive character when Russell is annoying Carl who, at that moment, is himself quite unfriendly. But beyond this, the boy's music, too, invades Carl's space.

The character, Charles Munz, adds a counter-theme—a versatile theme that transforms. It appears in the scene before the credits, accompanied by images of the explorer and his dirigible (*The Spirit of Adventure*) and is also the initial theme, while the young Carl walks along with his balloon recalling his hero. Here, the theme is positive in every sense and has the virtue of being easily remembered, ensuring that the audience will not forget it. It will not appear again until halfway through the film when Munz' chatting dogs have captured Carl, the child Russell and Dug, the dog, and taken them to the old explorer's hide-out. As they reach the dirigible we hear Munz' music diegetically (from a gramophone), marking out the territory into which they are entering. The theme in this variation maintains a similar meaning but when Munz turns out to be perverse and manipulative the theme also removes its mask and changes radically, becoming a sinister, menacing and hostile counter-theme. It will maintain this meaning for the rest of the film to become especially powerful in the final struggle between Charles and Carl, where this will be transferred to the music in the battle between the main theme/counter-theme until this latter disappears.[42]

These are the three themes on which the music script of *Up* is constructed. There is a lot more music with secondary themes but none of them hinders the advance of those three themes. Two of the themes are complex (the main theme and that of Munz which are designed to confront each other) and the other is very simple, put there purely to entertain.

How to Train Your Dragon, another animated film, has a music script where, along with many secondary themes, three central themes are developed, one of which is finally wiped out by the main theme. As in *Up*, the main theme plays a key role in the film. This theme represents the union between the young Hiccup and the dragon. It starts off as a derivative fragment, as a kind of code, accompanying the production house logo at the beginning of the film to continue building and gaining strength as the relationship between the two characters grows into something solid after an initial distrust. The theme begins as such in the scene where Hiccup takes a fish to the dragon, which is when their friendship begins and, as they get to know each other better, it fills out and develops. Although the theme is not yet sufficiently strong or important, in the awkward test-flight they take together, this provides a step forward leading up to the moment when, during that flight, they have to act as one in order to survive. It is at this moment when the theme reaches its full potential, expanding and finally ending. The question arises now that as the theme reaches its zenith at this point, only halfway into the film, and given that it will still have to show up again on other occasions, is it now condemned to maintain this full level of strength all the time, unable to grow even more? Will there be no way now for it to go beyond that magical moment?

The answer is "No". The main theme has another destiny which will make it even greater and more splendid, absorbing more characters into itself and taking up the space of other central themes, which it will end up wiping out. The first victim is the central theme

---

[42] In the closing credits, as final theme accompanied by the other central themes, it recovers its joy and sense of adventure, which has no other logic than to take away the drama and end up on a lighter note which, in terms of the story, makes no sense at all.

relating to Astrid, the Viking girl. This is not a theme for the character but for her emotion, which is romantic. It appears in the film's first scene when she comes out radiant from an explosion caused by the dragons. Linking the theme with her in this very physical and obvious fashion generates expectation around the importance she will have in how the film develops. The second time it appears is during the romantic flight of Hiccup and Astrid on the dragon's back. She is invited to make this flight but as yet is not part of the Hiccup-dragon crew. Therefore, the music deals with her emotion at the character's spatial level. However, this theme suddenly disappears and is replaced by the main theme. Now she is caught in the magic generated by Hiccup and the dragon and is just one more of them. After this, the various appearances of this theme are clearly of minor importance. In other words, while the main theme continues to grow, the central Astrid theme will go on diminishing. The same thing happens with the Vikings' central theme, a very simple theme that appears a number of times and that, in spite of its great musical strength, is quite elementary. The theme, always emphatic and forceful, is applied to the Viking clan and their struggle with the dragons. Along with its variations, it will also be applied to Hiccup when his attitude is that of a Viking warrior or aspires to be one. However, after the final battle, when Hiccup is left mutilated after killing the gigantic dragon and the whole village comes to see him, what we hear is the splendid main theme and not the theme of the Vikings. This music, initially shared by two characters, now belongs collectively to the whole community. This is another example of the power wielded by the main theme.

There is a notable example of good musical construction in a recent and successful Spanish film, *El Orfanato* (*The Orphanage*. J. A. Bayona. 2007) by Fernando Velázquez. The film tells the story of a woman's desperate search for her son who has mysteriously disappeared from the mansion where they live—an old orphanage where she herself grew up. More and more convinced that her son is *on the other side* (that he is dead), from where she receives signals from other children, she does everything possible to find him again. Although the film could be classed as a thriller, it is really a film about love—the unswerving love of a mother ready to renounce everything (including her own life) if, by doing so, she could again be with her lost son. The composer wrote two central themes for the film. The first was that of the mother (not Laura the character but the concept of motherhood and all it implies). The second theme, more difficult to categorize, was the theme of Death, of the other world. This was more generic and would serve to warn the audience about what was taking place on *the other side*. There are other themes, too, but all of them are secondary.

In a scene before the opening credits where Laura as a child is playing with the other children in the garden of the orphanage before being told she is going to be adopted, we hear the theme that later will become the melodic reference of *the other side*. This is a subtle warning of what is to come later, as we will eventually see her meet these children again at the end of the film. It is music that evokes a happy childhood, albeit one that is destroyed. All the children will be killed and they will take this music with them to the space of death. As the initial theme, the credit titles incorporate a fragment derived from this theme, which fuses with another derivative fragment to evolve into the mother theme. From this moment on and in all the narrative process of the film, both themes will move independently in their own direction: the theme of *the other side*, afflicted and often transforming, will express different levels of anguish, which refer to the suffering connected with *the other side;* while the mother theme, which will vary at times but will only be transformed in the final scene prior to the epilogue, will remain essentially music at the spatial level of the character's emotions, as well as at the spatial level of references. In that final scene, Laura finds out the truth and decides to commit suicide. She wakes up on *the other side* where her son is waiting for her and where she discovers all those children she played with as a child, who have been sending her so many clues during the film. This theme transforms in order to reach its maximum level of relief and peace, all very beautiful. However, it is clear that Laura does not belong to this space of death seeing that she is a new arrival. One of the children, going up to her and seeing her, exclaims: "It's Laura!" At that moment the mother theme comes in sounding strong and quite magnificent. Suddenly, Laura reigns over the entire space and the message transmitted by the transformation and the expansion of the mother theme is that she accepts her new situation and is, in turn, accepted by the children as their new mother. This dramatic moment, an absolute expression of love, could never have been achieved if the two central themes had not been well defined from the very beginning. The main theme, of course, is that of the mother which ends up dominating the space of the other central theme.

6.4. Musical silence

In order to define the discourse of the music script one must decide what characters or concepts will be involved in the music. As mentioned earlier, to deprive a character of music, while others have their own, may help to weaken that character (as seen in *Vertigo*), to lessen the character's importance so as to increase it for others who do have music (*Taxi Driver*), but also to strengthen it (as in *Pan's Labyrinth*). It all depends on individual circumstances and on what one wants to achieve. Apart from this, we should not discount the power of musical silence, which refers not only to those parts where no music is added because it is not useful or necessary, but especially to its absence in those places where, *a priori*, it seems necessary or the spectator is waiting to hear it. This must be understood in the sense that its absence is something decided beforehand, as when, for example, one wants to emphasize a sensation of emptiness or absence. Aaron Copland once said: *"Personally, I prefer to make use of music's power sparingly, saving it for absolutely essential points. A composer knows how to play with silences, knows that to take music out can at times be more effective than any use of it might be.*[43] On the other hand, Nino Rota felt that *"it is better that films have mediocre music rather than not have music at all. Musical silence leaves the spectator dissatisfied"*.[44] In any case, the fact is that the lack of music in a sequence may make it more powerful, either because of the contrast with what goes just before or after, when there was music or not, or because without music you might surprise the audience, accustomed to hearing music in such scenes. One of the best known examples is the chase of a crop-spraying airplane over Cary Grant in *North By Northwest*, a fragment that without music was way more effective, so much so that the director used the same effect again in *Torn Curtain* (1966) in the murder sequence in the kitchen. Another notable case is *Jaws,* as explained earlier regarding the scene where

---

[43] Thomas, T.: Op. Cit. P.77.

[44] Latorre, J.M.: «Nino Rota, La imagen de la música» (Montesinos, 1989) P.261.

one of the protagonists throws meat into the sea hoping the shark might show signs of life. Suddenly, without any warning from the music, the enormous shark appears and frightens both the protagonists and the audience. Immediately afterwards —but after— the music reappears. The effect is powerful because it takes the audience completely by surprise. A composer then has to know how to manage the possibilities offered by the absence of music. In *How to Train Your Dragon*, for example, it is highly significant that the relation of the father to the son is always with musical silence, up until the father realizes that his son is not the stupid useless person he thought he was.

6.5. How, where and why?

Having established the first criteria, determined the genetic codes of the central themes and made a selection of what will go into the music script and what is to be rejected, it is now time to put order to it all and avoid chaos. It is time to write the music script.

If you plan to construct a soundtrack with a bold structure, you must decide first of all what spaces the main theme needs to occupy. As it is the most important theme, you must assign it its moments and define its discourse: where it should come in complete, when fragmented, when repeated, varied or transformed, etc. Where, how and above all, why. It must always be justified and have a *raison-d'être*. You need to know how a scene or a character is going to benefit from this music. That is, unless it is going to be put in as a sub-theme of another, is sharing a space (for example, a scene with a musical duel as theme/counter-theme), or if the spaces where it is used are already occupied, even when, by narrative logic, those spaces correspond to another central theme.

Next you will go on to the other central themes, by order of importance, so that it will be relatively easy to see if the film is beginning to show signs of over-saturation, in which case it would be wise to eliminate one of the central themes so that the film might breathe easier. Keeping in mind that the secondary themes do not need the audience's intellectual participation, there is no problem in finding a place for them in the film. The most dangerous saturation is that which affects the comprehension of a film, not simply whether something might be heard or not. In a film whose music script has to play with various central themes, it is advisable that not all of them (unless there are only a few) have their own transformations, because this can lead to confusion. In this respect, it would be much better to stick to what is essential. It is infinitely more desirable to sacrifice something than to regret it later on. Therefore, a music scriptwriter must be able to respond to the following questions, although not necessarily in this order:

1. Over what dramatic levels is the music score going to move? Which are the most relevant?
2. Does the story level of the music correspond to that of the film?
3. Will existing music be used? Why?
4. If diegetic music is to be applied, will it be for narrative reasons or will it bring some other narrative or dramatic benefit? Will there be transitions? Will there be false diegesis?
5. What will be the main theme? And the central themes? Is there a counter-theme? Will there be an initial and/or a final theme? Will these be individual, shared or collective themes? Will any of these be expansive?
6. Will there be songs? Why?
7. In the main, central, initial and final themes:
    – What is the genetic code that makes them unique? What degree of integration do they have?
    – Which will be repeated and when? Which will be varied or transformed? Why and when?
    – When and why will they establish an emotional or intellectual communication?
    – In relation to what will they be empathetic?
    – In what spatial levels of the emotions will they be placed?

- Will they be used at the spatial level of references? And will they be used in that of music that has been introduced earlier?
- Will any of these work as a sub-theme of another? By reference or by dominion?
- Will derived or derivative motifs be made of them? Fragments? Leit-motifs?
8. Secondary themes: what will they be needed them for?
9. What music will be put in the spatial level of the action?
10. At what moments is it better that the music be listened to and when is it enough that it be heard? Will any theme block out the ambient sound?

It is possible that some of these questions do not need an answer—for example, if there are not going to be sub-themes or songs, diegesis, etc. But some of them are fundamental and need to be addressed in order to control what is wanted in the music script. It is possible that some of the answers may well be found in the literary script or in the film itself, without having to think much about them. Using these guidelines, all that is needed is to manage these elements conveniently, define a strategy and, in principle, the music script will be all laid out. Then, of course, the music must be written, orchestrated, recorded, edited and synchronized with the movie, making sure it remains compatible with the dialogue.

6.6. Music and dialogue

So long as we are not dealing with a silent film, the music must be made compatible with the dialogue. Music can strengthen dialogue or support it but there is always the danger that it may interfere with the flow of the words, distract attention from them or become redundant. Where music and dialogue have to share the same space, the validity of a sequence depends on the balance between them. It is important to remember that music will always take second place to words because dialogue—in principle, self-explanatory—will always play the leading role, not needing music to be understood. Nevertheless, there are times when the addition of music may add a broader dimension to dialogue. A very simple example is when the music strengthens or adds force to what is being said. For instance, when along with words of love a melody establishes a romantic and emotional setting; or when, in a stressful situation with tense dialogue, music can produce an even greater impression of unease. In such cases or similar ones, the score may not add anything new or different but it can add intensity as its effect is purely emotional. With music, a sentiment expressed in words may be extended and prolonged in the footage without needing to resort again to dialogue. That is to say, when music is used in a scene where the protagonists express a specific sentiment, it is enough to repeat or transform that music in another space so that, in essence, the words are repeated without our having to hear them again. The music has had a precise, emotional reference, which later becomes an intellectual link connecting the spectator with the previous scene when that melody came up for the first time, thus making unnecessary redundant dialogue. The very act of linking music with specific dialogue makes the music more expressive. If it extends into the space beyond the dialogue, its usefulness is notable as we see in the case of the main or central themes. Of course, it can happen that a theme is limited to a particular sequence and will not be used again.

When applying music in scenes with dialogue, one must consider the importance of the sound levels. The compatibility of music and words takes place on a level of sound equality in the case of songs, music in diegesis and music in general. However, sequences with dialogue demand to be understood and thus being able to hear the words must take priority. For this reason the music usually plays a subordinate role at a lower sound level than that of the voice when music and words occupy the same physical space in a film. When this is not the case because, for example, the actors stop speaking for a moment, the music may increase its sound level without causing problems. Let us look at three examples:

Example 1: music aids the dialogue without interfering with it. To some extent, music sometimes acts as a cushion over which the dialogue can flow smoothly and, what is more important, can help it to be heard. This is an advantage because music may even lighten what is being said so that it becomes more accessible. Let us consider a sequence with dialogue where there is no music and then think of the same sequence with music applied. In the first case, the audience will have to pay special attention so as not to miss any detail of what is being said because the words are the only sound reference. In the second case, while the audience will also have to pay attention, it will be more difficult for them to be distracted because the music has a powerful psychological effect that makes it possible for the words, at a good sound level, to flow more easily.

For this reason, many sequences of dialogue are accompanied by a musical background applied purely to make the words more telling. It does not matter if the music is incidental or diegetic, but in static scenes with dialogue (with characters sitting around a table and talking) the music is usually diegetic because it does not require any justification, whereas with incidental music there is the risk that the spectator may wonder where, in a fixed, specific location, the music is coming from. This does not happen in non-static scenes (with characters speaking while they are walking or moving around) because there are other visual elements which make them more dynamic—a change of scenery or the movement of the actors. In these cases, music may simply be one more element within the scene. In static scenes, even if the characters are silent, camera movement may drive the sequence and facilitate the addition of incidental music. Naturally, it is not essential there be music in a scene with dialogue and, if there is, it does not have to be heard all through the sequence, although in this case, if used incidentally, care should be taken with the breaks in the music. They must be coherent, not be noticeable nor disturb the rhythm of the sequence.

Example 2: the music does not interfere with the dialogue but, when there is no dialogue, the sound level increases in order to take a more prominent role which it abandons when the dialogue resumes. This is a method often used in which more importance is given to the music, making it more of a protagonist than in Case 1, where it simply accompanied the scene and its dialogue. In this case, the functional utility (music to sustain the spoken word) alternates with the dramatic. Obviously, this is not just a technical matter of raising or lowering the volume because this would be too forced and, furthermore, would draw attention to the music unless, of course, the composer knew how to adjust the two sound levels to ensure a coherent and aesthetic result. This, logically enough, cannot be done with diegetic music given that it would not make sense nor have any justification.

Example 3: even if there should be interruptions in the dialogue, the music does not change its sound level but maintains a similar tone throughout the whole sequence, never playing a leading role. This is the inevitable resource whenever diegetic music is used but it is also valid with incidental music if, for whatever reason, it is not intended to give the music any dramatic emphasis. As in the first case, it is not essential that the music be heard all through the sequence, but if it is used incidentally, care must be taken that the breaks in the music be coherent.

If the music openly interferes with the dialogue, without any apparent coordination, it hampers the flow and understanding of the words. It is important to repeat that where a scene has words and music, the words will always have priority. If they do not, they should be dispensed with. When linked to dialogue, music can do much more than simply regulate or accompany it, by giving it a broader meaning than that expressed in the words. For example, in a declaration of love, a romantic melody will emphasize what is being said. However, if the music is sad it may put a quite different perspective on this declaration of love, changing the meaning of the dialogue completely. The music needs to be linked to the dialogue not only to accompany it but to make it more exact for the audience. The words and music have need of each other to ensure that the audience is able to understand the real dimension of the emotions expressed by the characters. The music serves to evoke what is being told in the dialogue: if a character mentions something that may be transcribed in the form of music, the presence of the melody will add to the narrative and dramatic dimension of the sequence. It then functions as a reference broadening the spatial field of the scene. It may even be used to reveal the fact that a character is lying. Imagine a person saying sweet words to another while accompanied by sinister music. We would think he was lying, or that he was going to kill him. Or, on the other hand, when a character is talking in trivialities to the sound of romantic music, we know he is in love but does not dare to say so. The music will always give the game away!

Another important aspect related to music and dialogue is when the latter comes in the form of voice-over relating events or facts. In such cases, so that music and voice are in accord and the combination is harmonious, it is usually more practical to record the voice according to the music and not the other way around: what is recited should be paced keeping in mind the flow of the music. In this way, moments of great beauty and precision can be achieved, as occurs in a good part of *The Age of Innocence* for which Elmer Bernstein wrote the music.[45]

6.7. Music and film sequences

Another aspect to keep in mind is the connection between sequences that music makes possible, the shifts of continuity or with ellipses (changes of tempo between one scene and another). These changes carried out with music may make them flow better and appear less brusque, so that they seem natural even when they involve the passing of years or a change of location. It is enough to take out the music in the final part of a scene and link it to the next, or end it in the first few seconds of a scene when it has already been heard in the previous scene.

Music may also help to join different sequences giving an impression of unity and continuity, despite jumps in time or space. It is worth remembering the phenomenal opening of *Citizen Kane* in which a succession of shots takes us to the protagonist as he is dying. Bernard Herrmann's music sets those initial shots and leads us to the moment of climax when the snowball Kane is holding falls to the ground and breaks up. Or think of the montage of sequences at the end of *The Godfather* that is solidly unified thanks to the music, despite the sharp contrast of these sequences—a killing and a wedding. A sequence is a series of images artificially joined together

---

[45] But this is not an absolute requirement because, as we have already seen, the composer can provide for the words and make them more harmonious, though this is, undoubtedly, more work. Even so, Dimitri Tiomkin and Georges Delerue did this, and very well, in The Old Man and the Sea (John Sturges, 1958) and in Les deux anglaises et le continent (Two English Girls, François Truffaut, 1971), respectively.

in the editing, and the music fuses these fragments into a single unit so that the spectator believes that it is a single compact sequence.

The beginning of *The Remains of the Day*, with music by Richard Robbins, consists of a long succession of shots, which explain a series of facts prior to the real beginning of the film's story: (the arrival at the mansion/auction of the mansion/butler opening mansion windows/butler taking breakfast tray/walking through passages carrying the tray/the new owner eating breakfast and talking to the butler). This chain of shots is accompanied by the same music. In this way, the important events are rapidly narrated in a fluid and natural manner thanks to the use of a single theme linking them together. Without music the changes would have been brusque. This system is very practical in films that begin with quick short explanations at the beginning in order to bring the audience to the specific point at which the story begins. In *Tom Jones*, with a score by John Addison, the same thing happens, In this case, it is done with Baroque music that explains the circumstances of the protagonist's origins.

We also find music used to unite disparate sequences in films where an attempt is made to give them a solid single tone, in spite of the narrative and time differences. One example of a succession of sequences where time is accelerated is to be seen in *The Age of Innocence*. Here, with the aid of Joanne Woodward's voice (which narrates the film), a long montage of sequences sets out, in a masterful and elegant manner, the sentimental evolution of the protagonists' life and marriage. In reality, Bernstein plays with two different themes, one after the other, which fuse together the ellipses and also facilitate a change of tone within the whole, thanks to the use of the two successive melodies.

Philip Glass, in *The Hours*, goes one step further and fuses together parallel sequences from three historical epochs—the Twenties, the Fifties and the present day. These different periods are not presented successively but are alternated and the composer gives them a solid homogeneous look so that the changes take place coherently. The film intermingles three stories, two about women readers of Virginia Woolf, and a third about the writer herself. The music helps these jumps in time seem natural, avoiding the sensation that they are three films in one, instead of a single film solidly intertwined. If the composer had written a theme for each period, or a different musical style for each historical period he would not have achieved this unity within the film. In that case, perfectly valid on the other hand, there would be three stories and the episodes would be quite independent. However, one music holds the film together, fuses the episodes and gives the film a natural and fluid continuity. It can also happen that, when a film narrates a story elliptically, the music can contribute to making a brief and condensed story flow easily and naturally. One of the most notable moments in *Ed Wood* is when the excited protagonist is interviewed by Orson Welles and decides to end the filming of what he believes will be the film of his life. What happens then is a montage of sequences which explains the creative process involved in the making of the film, up to its presentation. This was a process that, in scarcely a few minutes, reduces what took weeks to happen. Howard Shore's music, with a highly emotional and accelerating crescendo, helps to unify such a jump in time. In *Todo sobre mi madre* (All About My Mother. Pedro Almodóvar, 1999), with music by Alberto Iglesias, two montages of elliptical sequences are employed one after the other.

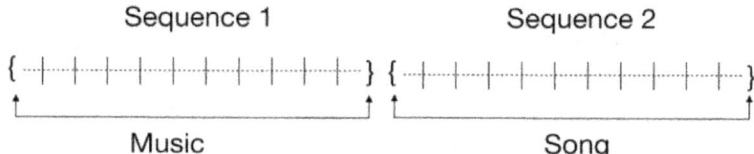

The first montage runs from when the protagonist signs the approval for the donation of her son's organs to when a patient is receiving those organs. The second begins when she starts out on a trip to Barcelona and ends when she reaches a vacant lot where she will meet with a transsexual. In the first montage there is a short explanation of what happens over a period of several days. In the second there is a resumé of what happens over hours. Both run practically one after the other, which could be somewhat disturbing if it were not eased by the insertion of distinct blocks of music (a musical theme and a song, respectively). The fact that each of these blocks, used to resolve the montage of the elliptical sequences, has a different music can be explained by the need to differentiate between them. This is logical enough as the events are different, but it also avoids the confusion that could arise if the music used in both cases were similar. As a result, they are clearly different and individual.

Within reasonable limits, a good music track can sustain a sequence beyond the bare story it tells and even extend its duration much farther than it would without such application. We have already seen how this was done in the case of *Per qualche dollaro in più*, but it is not necessary to resort to tricks. The most important thing is that, if you want to extend a sequence, you must have some justification for doing so—either to emphasize something, to generate tension or to take advantage of the visual or dramatic richness of the scene itself. A very simple way to lengthen a sequence is to slow it down and make the image run slower than normal and thus last longer. If the music also seems to be slowed down, the obvious effect is that the same thing is being explained but over a longer time. This is what happens in the final scenes of *Obsession* and *Carrie* (both by Brian De Palma and both filmed in 1976) in which the scores by Bernard Herrmann and Pino Donaggio match the rhythm of images in slow-motion, thereby converting some sequences into longer segments which in normal circumstances would last a very short time. Throughout his career, Herrmann himself used a more subtle formula to extend the duration of a scene and, in his case, to cause unease. He did so with unresolved music which seemed as if it might go on forever. When it gave the impression it had ended, it started up again in circular repetitions where, having reached a specific point, the music would go back to the beginning, and so on indefinitely. This we can see in the initial theme of *Vertigo,* in the sequence on Rushmore mountain in *North By Northwest* or in *Taxi Driver*, among others, with melodies without any logical resolution but which wear themselves out. Repeated several times they give the impression they are never going to end and when it seems they have finally got somewhere they go back to their starting point. In terms of cinema, it works very well indeed. The disturbing static impression naturally provokes a great deal of anguish because in such situations we are waiting for an ending that will provide relief and allow us to relax and feel that *this has finally ended.* But Herrmann did not do this and as a result he managed to maintain and extend whole sequences almost indefinitely.

If the music is pleasing, it is usually difficult to object to its presence, even when the action has ended. We can see how music is

6. The Music Script

very much at home in any film that includes beautiful scenes—in *Dances with Wolves* (Kevin Costner, 1990)—or, it goes without saying, in films with scarcely any dialogue. In these cases, the camera can hold longer in order to show nature scenes or follow characters walking through beautiful countryside because the music serves as a reinforcing factor and the audience is more patient if they are enjoying what they are seeing and hearing. In a similar way, the construction sequence that takes place on the farm in *Witness* (Peter Weir, 1985) is put together according to the music by Maurice Jarre, and not the other way around, so that it can be longer than it would normally be. The same thing happens in car chases in police films and the like, which naturally rest on frantic action but where, supported by suitable musical accompaniment, can be extended so that they take up more time without the risk of appearing overdone. The intense chase scenes in *Bullitt* (Peter Yates, 1968) were filmed in large measure thanks to the Lalo Schifrin's music.

If the music manages to be more suggestive or emotional than the scene where it is applied (and this may be what is intended), the spectator will rarely object that the sequence go on as long as the music lasts because it will be welcome. There are times when the melody is even more important than the picture itself for establishing a specific location. This is generally because what is being narrated with images is elementary or minimal but the mediation of music can make it broader, transcendent or intense. In *Dressed to Kill* (Brian De Palma, 1980), for example, there is a very long scene in a museum where all that happens is a woman and a man exchange glances and follow each other through the galleries and passageways. With the score by Pino Donaggio there develops a feeling of growing desire and passion along with a certain intrigue which increases as the sequence develops. There is very little action and the scene would become dreary if it were not for the intervention of the music that makes its lengthy duration viable and easy to sit through. For just as music can draw out a scene, it can also give it greater intensity or more life either by extending the sequence, or not.

A classical example of this is to be found in *The Magnificent Seven* that would be much too slow without music, or *Lawrence of Arabia* where there is a sequence of special significance, that of the man who has fainted in the desert and the protagonist saves him, risking his own life. As the young camp lookout becomes surprised to realize that the imperceptible form on the horizon is that of Lawrence, the tone of the music increases progressively until it reaches its fullest ecstasy with their meeting, when it reaches levels of splendour and emotion seldom achieved in film history. The key to this moment, as well as the music itself, was the correct decision of the director and the composer to begin the first chords of the theme a little ahead of the action in the scene, so that the music was already taking part in the euphoria of the moment before this had could be seen. In a more concentrated sense, a brief but intense sequence can become even stronger with the right music. An essential reference is the scene just before the arrival of the "baddies" in *High Noon* where shots of a clock are interspersed with the reaction of concern or fear of all the characters in the film. The sequence is telling and very powerful in itself because of its impeccable editing but really gains on all fronts through the powerful and unrelenting music of Dimitri Tiomkin, which—in a brief period of time—generates enormous tension.

There are more subtle options which arise from the synchronous relationship between camera movement and music. What is normal in camera movement is that the music mark the time of what is being shown so that, in a sense, it runs behind the visual. This is what happens at the beginning of *Psycho* where the music accompanies a travelling shot taking us inside a motel. When the reverse takes place, that is, when the camera follows the music and we hear it before we see the visual, the intensifying effect becomes quite clear and what the camera is trying to show becomes much more important. We see this in the first moments of *Citizen Kane,* when the music takes the spectator by the hand from a wide shot of the Kane mansion up to the crystal ball. And also in the sequence in the house of the film magnate in *The Godfather,* starting out from a wide shot of the house when we hear the first chords of the main theme, indicating that the Padrino's thugs have been there to carry out their revenge. As the music heightens, the camera moves in closer until it reaches the bed of the magnate who discovers the head of his horse between the sheets. It is the music that carries the spectator, while the camera simply follows the path set out with the result that the action is greatly intensified.

6.8. When should the music be written?

A matter that has generated much debate and continues to do so centres on when the music score should be written: should this be done even before the film is shot? During the shoot? Or does a composer have to see the final film shot and edited before starting to work? Before dealing with each of these possibilities, we ought to make clear that in the history of cinema extraordinary scores have been written in all three periods (before, during and after). Furthermore, and this is perhaps most important, what really matters is the result. If a film score is good, what does it matter when it was written? In most cases, however, it is not the composer who decides when to start his work on the film. Although it might be reasonable to think that the sooner he starts, the better, this is not always possible.[46]

Let us look at specific cases in which it is almost imperative that the music be written before, during or after the film has been shot, although the process initiated before the film has begun usually goes on right to its very end.

1.– Music written before the film shoot

There are factors that make it necessary to write the music before shooting the film. One clearly obvious factor involves the songs in a musical film, but there are others—for instance, music that is to be interpreted diegetically or is needed because a character refers specifically to it. These are not the only examples; it could happen that while a character appears to be playing music it may well be written after the sequence has been filmed, although it is more practical to write it beforehand. There are also cases where one wants to dedicate a sequence to the power of the music, in which case it is probably useful to be able to plan the sequence already knowing the music. The entire final scene in *The Red Shoes* (Michael Powell,

---

[46] "If music (the mystery) was a part of early production, rather than postproduction, it would be far less intimidating. Early on there would still be time and money with which to fix or audition. But, with the film all done and either working or not working and the delivery date lurking in the all too foreseeable future, it is not the best time to be adding an element which only one person in the room fully understands" (Bellis, R. Op. Cit. P. 67).

Emeric Pressburger, 1948), for example, is a ballet with music by Brian Easdale which was certainly written before being filmed. However, if there is a fine example of a director wanting to have the music written before shooting his film and a composer who fully understood his reasons, it was Sergio Leone whose films all had music by Ennio Morricone. There were two basic reasons for doing this, both of which were important. First of all, having the music beforehand allowed complete scenes to be planned according to the music so that they seemed to have been *choreographed* and were very beautiful. Secondly, because Leone always felt the music to be a natural extension of the characters, making them more understandable and giving them a broader, more ethereal, almost religious dimension. What is more, if an actor needed to know his lines beforehand in order to understand his character, why should he not also know the music that was going to be his character's *soul*? For this reason, Leone made his actors listen to Morricone's music.

2.– Music written during shooting of the film

In a sequence of *La nuit américaine,* Truffaut's secretary receives a telephone call which is passed to the director. He is told it is Georges Delerue. *Hello, Georges,* says Truffaut. *I have the music for the film. Do you want to hear it?* ask the composer. *Yes, play it for me*, replies the director. The music is played over the phone and Truffaut says: *Great, Georges. I'm very pleased. Thank you.* Then he hungs up. This film, representative of *film-within-a-film* showed the process of shooting a film and the participation of a composer in that process. Here, while the director is filming, the composer is writing. Just as a script may change as the filming goes on, the composer has the opportunity to rewrite or make changes along the way aware that his script will have to be adjusted to the final film. To some extent, film and music merge together so long as the composer can see the footage filmed or be present at the shoot. The parallel creation of the music has many advantages and sets few problems given that the composer may have access to first-hand information, time and—even more important—be able to make suggestions. In the editing room he can adjust his music and, if this has been created while following the development of the film from the beginning, everything will be much simpler and easier. A composer who knows his business can help a director make important decisions, such as cutting out unnecessary dialogue, simplifying ellipses, transitions or any other resource in which he may be able to take an active part. That is, of course, if and when the director is open to his suggestions. In these circumstances, the composer may obtain stimulus from the film in process and be able to include these in what he writes. After all, as director Robert Aldrich pointed out: "*I think that the musician is an extension of the director*".[47]

Because of all such contributions it is very useful to have a composer at work on a film at an early stage. This makes it possible during the shoot to be able to edit parts of the film in keeping with the music. The composer may have written his music following a first edit or a sketch of it and then during the final edit he may be asked to adjust the music or the editor may be asked to change what he has done. This happened in *Citizen Kane* and in *E.T. The Extra-Terrestrial* and in *The Age of Innocence* with sequences edited in keeping with the music and not the other way around.[48]

3.– Music written after filming

Unfortunately, it happens too often that a film is shot and edited and then someone remembers it needs music. It is then they rush to find a composer and ask him to work quickly and efficiently to create a miracle because a release date has already been set. At times like this someone is liable to announce they need the music for yesterday and this is the nightmare of any composer. There are times when there is no other way than to work with the final edit because adjustments must be timed precisely to the very second. This happens in animation films even though the music could have been written beforehand. The key to music written after the film is edited depends on the time allowed the composer. While it is true that a composer cannot at this stage make significant suggestions, it is possible that those missed proposals were not really so necessary. At other times, of course, they

---

[47] Karlin, F.: Op. Cit. P.12.

[48] With regard to The Age of Innocence, Elmer Bernstein told me: "When I finished my work (Scorsese) began to edit parts of the film in keeping with the music, as took place in the wedding sequences, the honeymoon and the segment dealing with the passage of time. As a result, there was a real marriage between picture and music. That is the best way to work."

might well benefit the film, as long as the composer has the time and the director is amenable.

Lack of time has long been the curse of composers. Once the filming is finished it is always hoped that post-production (including the soundtrack) will be rapidly completed. The main difficulty most Hollywood composers had to deal with in the Thirties and Forties was the vast amount of work commissioned with little time available—a difficult situation that remained unchanged with few exceptions right up to the end of the days of the big studios in the Fifties. Max Steiner, for example, left RKO for this reason but things did not improve. Perhaps he was exaggerating when he talked about his staggering work on Gone with the Wind (Victor Fleming, 1939): *"I wrote the 3 hours and 45 minutes of original music for* Gone with the Wind, *plus the score for another film and supervised the recording of both, and within the space of four weeks... I did it by getting exactly 15 hours of sleep during those four weeks and working steadily the rest of the time. You can't be a Beethoven under these conditions"*.[49] Dimitri Tiomkin also suffered the same thing. *"Four weeks was all I was allowed to write the The Alamo (John Wayne, 1960) score. The Guns of Navarone (J.Lee Thompson, 1961), it is five weeks. It is ruining my health and my heart"*.[50] Victor Young was more pragmatic: *"Why indeed, would any trained musician let himself in for a career that calls for the exactitude of an Einstein, the diplomacy of Churchill, and the patience of a martyr. Yet, after doing some 350 film scores, I can think of no other musical medium that offers as much challenge, excitement, and demand for creativity in putting music to work"*.[51]

The presence of arrangers to do the orchestration helped and continues to help ease the difficulties and economize on time. Hans J. Salter describes things this way: *"Those people who feel that composers do their own orchestrations should have been at Universal (in the Forties). There simply was no time for such luxuries"*.[52] In principle, no one spoke about authorship. *"If I dictate a letter and it is*

---

[49] Karlin, F.: Op.cit. p.192.

[50] Bona, D. y Wiley, M.: «Inside Oscar» (Ballantine Books, 1986) P. 322.

[51] Thomas,T.: Op.cit. p. 162. Young died of a heart attack when he was only 56.

[52] Karlin, F.: Op.cit. p.35.

typed for me, who actually wrote the letter, me or my secretary?" asked Aaron Copland.[53] Of course, there were and still are differences of criteria on this matter. As a result, while there are composers who work with a team of arrangers other composers do not. In my discussions with composers I have come across opinions of all kinds.[54]

The music then has to pass through the decisions taken in the editing room and the laying in of other sound elements. If the composer is not present in this process his work may well suffer the consequences. There have been any number of occasions when the laying in of sound effects has become a real drama. These effects, so essential, must be combined with the music with the result that often there is a constant struggle to gain weight in a sequence. A bad mix can destroy any music score, drown it by sound effects. Every composer knows that the decisions made at this stage may mean there are themes that finally are not used. But it has happened that at this delicate moment a decision is taken to make drastic cuts or even to do away with a score completely. This happened to David Raksin with Carrie (William Wyler, 1952) as he explained: *"there was a final sequence, near seven minutes long, and almost without dialogue. I knew than Willie Wyler, the director, was going to shorten it; so, since we were working on an impossible time schedule, I asked him to spare me the necessity of composing more music than we would actually use. He said he couldn't cut the sequence until he saw it with the music. So I wrote the sequence –it inspired some of the best music I*

---

[53] Previn, A.: «No Minor Chords: My Days in Hollywood» (Doubleday, 1991). P.89

[54] Morricone is adamant about what he considers a composer's integrity. In the book «Morricone, la música, el cine» (Fundación Municipal de Cine de Valencia, 1997), the author, Sergio Miceli, asked him if he had ever used collaborators: "Never, it is a moral principle that cannot be waived. I like to compose, it is my vocation, the only thing I know how to do. I cannot delegate to others an obligation I profoundly consider my own." He also mentioned personal reasons: "I began in this profession being responsible for orchestration and arrangements for musicians who were well paid while I had nothing (...), that is to say, I was exploited and I cannot do the same to others for moral reasons but also for artistic reasons." He added: Some well-known composers of film music use this type of collaboration. This is something I just do not understand because even if you hand in a well-resolved and very clear fragment, the orchestration is the music. The fact you put 'bridge' or 'pizzicato' for the viola forms part of the music and has an influence on the entire sound. For me, therefore, it is unacceptable as a principle, not only moral but also artistic. The creator of the music is who writes it from beginning to end, for better or worse." (P.103 and 104).

have ever composed- and there was joy over the place. Then they cut the sequence down to something like 56 seconds, and with that they destroyed the music".[55] Erich Wolfgang Korngold made a brilliant comment: "*A film composer's immortality stretches all the way from the recording stage to the dubbing room*".[56] This need not be inevitable if everyone involved in the process understands the importance of the music script from the time it is written until it is finally applied.

---

[55] Karlin, F.: Op.cit. p.63.

[56] Karlin, F.: Op. cit. P. 56.

7. Final Words

Putting music to a film is easy. Find a composer, ask for music and lay it into the film. Any composer can do it. However, preparing a music script that is going to prove adequate is another calling and much more exciting. At the beginning of this book, I made clear that *the composer who does not propose solutions is one who simply follows instructions*. Adolph Deutsch defined the work of a film composer with irony*: "A film composer is like a funeral-home employee. He cannot bring back to life a dead film but he is expected to make it look more presentable"*.[57] A music script will certainly not resuscitate a dead film but at least it will be able to give it a whiff of breath and make it run with more vigour. It is enough to add order to it and to ably move the pieces of the musical chess game.

This is not easy. The film composer must be a negotiator, a diplomat as well as a saint, to be able to deal patiently with the opinions and decisions he will come up against. Furthermore, he must also be a good sportsman to surmount the obstacles he might well encounter along the way—the director, the producer, the editor, the mixer of the music (especially if they know nothing about music). The best way to negotiate, to be diplomatic and not need so much patience is to have arguments that explain the need for music, rather than merely trusting in music's power to create emotion or to please. This latter option is risky because other people's judgment about music will always be subjective. It is also advisable not to take them into the music terrain where they will possibly feel insecure. Instead, it is best to help them visualize and comprehend the music so that they may see it as a narrative element. If they are able to understand the meaning that is to be given to the music and the value it will have for the film, the whole creative process will very likely turn out to be simpler. The purpose of this book is to provide a starting point for those composers so that they may become film-makers and feel themselves to be so. This is something quite different from what often happens and is certainly a much more desirable goal.

---

[57] Thomas, T.: «Music for the Movies» (Silman-James Pr. 1997). P. 18-19.

8. Aforementioned Films

2001: A Space Odyssey (Stanley Kubrick, 1968)

Abrazos rotos, Los (Broken Embraces. Pedro Almodóvar, 2009)

Adventures of Robin Hood, The (Michael Curtiz, William Keighley, 1938)

Age of Innocence, The (Martin Scorsese, 1993)

Agnes of God (Norman Jewison, 1985)

Alamo, The (John Wayne, 1960)

Alexis Zorba (Zorba the Greek. Michael Caccoyannis, 1964)

Alfie (Lewis Gilbert, 1966)

Altered States (Ken Russell, 1980)

Amadeus (Milos Forman, 1984)

Amarcord (Federico Fellini, 1974)

American Beauty (Sam Mendes, 1999)

Amistad (Steven Spielberg, 1997) 44

Anatomy of a Murder (Otto Preminger, 1959)

Argo (Ben Affleck, 2012)

Around the World in 80 Days (Michael Anderson, 1956)

Artist, The (Michel Hazanavicius, 2011)

Ascenseur pour l'échafaud (Elevator to the Gallows. Louis Malle, 1957)

Atonement (Joe Wright, 2007)

Aviator, The (Martin Scorsese, 2004)

Basic Instinct (Paul Verhoeven, 1992) 114

Batman (Tim Burton, 1989)

Ben-Hur (William Wyler, 1959)

Birds, The (Alfred Hitchcock, 1963)

Blade Runner (Ridley Scott, 1982)

Body Heat (Lawrence Kasdan, 1981)

Borgia, Los (Antonio Hernández, 2006)

Braveheart (Mel Gibson, 1995)

Breakfast at Tiffany's (Blake Edwards, 1961)

Bride of Frankenstein, The (James Whale, 1935)

Bridge Too Far, A (Richard Attenborough, 1977)

Bullitt (Peter Yates, 1968)

Buono, il brutto, il cattivo, Il (The Good, the Bad, the Ugly. Sergio Leone, 1966)

C'era una volta il west (Once Upon a Time in the West. Sergio Leone, 1968)

Caine Mutiny, The (Edward Dmytryck, 1954)

Carrie (William Wyler, 1952)

Carrie (Brian De Palma, 1976)

Casablanca (Michael Curtiz, 1943)

Catch Me If You Can (Steven Spielberg, 2002)

Chariots of Fire (Hugh Hudson, 1981)

8. Aforementioned Films

Choristes, Les (The Chorus. Christophe Barratier, 2004)

Citizen Kane (Orson Welles, 1941)

Clockwork Orange, A (Stanley Kubrick, 1971) 40

Close Encounters of the Third Kind (Steven Spielberg, 1977)

Cloud Atlas (Tom Tykwer, Andy & Lana Wachowski, 2012)

Commitments, The (Alan Parker, 1991)

Coraline (Henry Selik, 2009)

Cotton Club, The (Francis Ford Coppola, 1984)

Creature from the Black Lagoon (Jack Arnold, 1954)

Dances With Wolves (Kevin Costner, 1990)

Dark Knight Rises, The (Christopher Nolan, 2012)

Dark Knight, The (Christopher Nolan, 2008)

Days of Wine and Roses (Blake Edwards, 1962)

Deux anglaises et le continent, Les (Two English Girls. François Truffaut, 1971)

Diary of Anne Frank, The (George Stevens, 1959)

District 9 (Neill Blomkamp, 2009)

Donnie Brasco (Mike Newell, 1997)

Double Indemnity (Billy Wilder, 1944)

Dracula (Tod Browning, 1932)

Dracula (Terence Fisher, 1958)

Dracula (John Badham, 1979)

Drag Me To Hell (Sam Raimi, 2009)

Dressed to Kill (Brian De Palma, 1980)

E.T. The Extra-Terrestrial (Steven Spielberg, 1982)

Ed Wood (Tim Burton, 1994)

Elephant Man, The (David Lynch, 1980)

Elizabeth (Shekhar Kapur, 1998) 24,

End of the Affair, The (Neil Jordan, 1999)

Evil Dead (Fede Álvarez, 2013) 13,

Fabuleux destin d´Amélie Poulain, Le (Amélie. Jean Pierre Jeunet, 2001)

Fall of the Roman Empire, The (Anthony Mann, 1964)

Far from Heaven (Todd Haynes, 2002)

Fargo (Joel Coen, 1996)

Fortunella (Eduardo De Filippo, 1958)

Frida (Julie Taymor, 2002) 62, 126, 131

Gandhi (Richard Attenborough, 1982)

Ghost Writer, The (Roman Polanski, 2010)

Girl with the Dragon Tattoo, The (David Fincher, 2011)

Gladiator (Ridley Scott, 2000)

Godfather, The (Francis Ford Coppola, 1972)

Godfather, Part II, The (Francis Ford Coppola, 1974)

Godfather, Part III, The (Francis Ford Coppola, 1990)

Godfellas (Martin Scorsese, 1990)

Gone with the Wind (Victor Fleming, 1939)

Good Night, and Good Luck (George Clooney, 2005)

Great Escape, The (John Sturges, 1963)

Guns of Navarone, The (J. Lee Thompson, 1961)

Havana (Sydney Pollack, 1990)

High Noon (Fred Zinnemann, 1952)

Hours, The (Stephen Daldry, 2002)

How to Train Your Dragon (Dean DeBlois, Chris Sanders, 2010)

Hush... Hush, Sweet Charlotte (Robert Aldrich, 1964)

Inception (Christopher Nolan, 2010)

Incredibles, The (Brad Bird, 2004)

Interiors (Woody Allen, 1978)

Jaws (Steven Spielberg, 1975)

Journey to the Center of the Earth (Henry Levin, 1959)

Juno (Jason Reitman, 2007)

King Kong (Ernst B. Schoedsack, Merian C. Cooper, 1933)

King Kong (Peter Jackson, 2005)

King's Speech, The (Tom Hooper, 2010)

Laberinto del Fauno, El (Pan's Labyrinth. Guillermo del Toro, 2006)

Laura (Otto Preminger, 1944)

Lawrence of Arabia (David Lean, 1962)

Life of Pi (Ang Lee, 2012)

Little Romance, A (George Roy Hill, 1979)

Lo imposible (The Impossible. J.A. Bayona, 2012)

Lord of the Rings, The (Peter Jackson, 2001-2003)

Magnificent Seven, The (John Sturges, 1960)

Magnolia (Paul Thomas Anderson, 1999)

Malcolm X (Spike Lee, 1992)

Malèna (Giuseppe Tornatore, 2000)

Man who Knew Too Much, The (Alfred Hitchcock, 1956)

Man with the Golden Arm, The (Otto Preminger, 1955)

Marie Antoinette (Sofia Coppola, 2006)

Mariée était en noir, La (The Bride Wore Black. François Truffaut, 1967)

Migliore offerta, La (The Best Offer. Giuseppe Tornatore, 2013)

Mission, The (Roland Joffé, 1986)

Munich (Steven Spielberg, 2005)

North By Northwest (Alfred Hitchcock, 1959)

Notes On a Scandal (Richard Eyre, 2006)

Nuit américaine, La (Day for Night. François Truffaut, 1973)

Obsession (Brian De Palma, 1976)

Old Man and The Sea, The (John Sturges, 1958)

Omen, The (Richard Donner, 1976)

One Flew Over the Cuckoo's Nest (Milos Forman, 1975)

One from the Heart (Francis Ford Coppola, 1982)

Orfanato, El (The Orphanage. J.A. Bayona, 2007)

Out of Africa (Sydney Pollack, 1985)

Papillon (Franklin J. Schaffner, 1973)

Passage to India, A (David Lean, 1984)

8. Aforementioned Films

Passion of the Christ, The (Mel Gibson, 2004)

Patton (Franklin J. Schaffner, 1970)

Peau douce, La (The Soft Skin. François Truffaut, 1964)

Per qualche dollaro in più (For a Few Dollars More. Sergio Leone, 1965)

Pinocchio (Ben Sharpsteen, Hamilton Luske, 1940)

Pinocchio (Roberto Benigni, 2002)

Planet of the Apes (Franklin J. Schaffner, 1968)

Platoon (Oliver Stone, 1986)

Postino, Il (The Postman. Michael Radford, 1995)

Psycho (Alfred Hitchcock, 1960)

Pulp Fiction (Quentin Tarantino, 1994)

Quo Vadis (Mervyn LeRoy, 1951)

Ragtime (Milos Forman, 1981)

Raiders of the Lost Ark (Steven Spielberg, 1981)

Red Shoes, The (Michael Powell, Emeric Pressburger, 1948)

Red Violin, The (François Girard, 1999)

Remains of the Day, The (James Ivory, 1993)

Rocky (John G. Avildsen, 1976)

Romeo and Juliet (Franco Zeffirelli, 1968)

Room with a View, A (James Ivory, 1986)

Rosemary's Baby (Roman Polanski, 1968)

Saving Private Ryan (Steven Spielberg, 1998)

Schindler's List (Steven Spielberg, 1993)

Se7en (David Fincher, 1995)

Sense and Sensibility (Ang Lee, 1995)

Shame (Steve McQueen, 2011)

Signs (M. Night Shyamalan, 2002)

Silence of the Lambs, The (Jonathan Demme, 1991)

Silent Movie (Mel Brooks, 1976)

Sixth Sense, The (M. Night Shyamalan, 1999)

Sleuth (Joseph L. Mankiewicz, 1972)

Spartacus (Stanley Kubrick, 1960)

Spellbound (Alfred Hitchcock, 1945)

Star Trek (J.J. Abrams, 2009)

Star Wars (George Lucas, 1977)

Star Wars. Episode V - The Empire Strikes Back (Irving Kershner, 1980)

Strangers on a Train (Alfred Hitchcock, 1951)

Sunset Boulevard (Billy Wilder, 1950)

Taxi Driver (Martin Scorsese, 1976)

Third Man, The (Carol Reed, 1949)

Titanic (James Cameron, 1997)

To Kill a Mockingbird (Alan J. Pakula, 1962)

Todo sobre mi madre (All About My Mother. Pedro Almodóvar, 1999)

Tom Jones (Tony Richardson, 1963)

Torn Curtain (Alfred Hitchcock, 1966)

Treasure of the Sierra Madre, The (John Huston, 1948)

Tucker: the Man and His Dream (Francis Ford Coppola, 1988)

8. Aforementioned Films

Two For the Road (Stanley Donen, 1967)

Unforgiven (Clint Eastwood, 1992)

Untouchables, The (Brian De Palma, 1987)

Up (Pete Docter, Bob Peterson, 2009)

Vangelo seccondo Matteo, Il (The Gospel According St. Matthew. Pier Paolo Pasolini, 1966)

Vertigo (Alfred Hitchcock, 1958)

Village, The (M. Night Shyamalan, 2004)

Viridiana (Luis Buñuel, 1959)

Viskningar och rop (Cries and Whispers. Ingmar Bergman, 1973)

Vita è bella, La (Life Is Beautiful. Roberto Benigni, 1998)

Walking Dead, The (series. 2010)

War Horse (Steven Spielberg, 2011)

Who's Afraid of Virginia Woolf? (Mike Nichols, 1966)

Witness (Peter Weir, 1985)

Woman Under the Influence, A (John Cassavetes, 1974)

Young Frankenstein (Mel Brooks, 1974)

Conrado Xalabarder

Conrado Xalabarder (Barcelona, Spain, 1964), renowned specialist in the field of film music, is the creator of MundoBSO.com, world's largest film music website. He is also film music critic in Fotogramas (Spain's most-read film magazine), and writes about film music for newspapers, magazines, etc.

Teacher of Film Music at the Universities Pompeu Fabra and Vic (both in Barcelona, Spain), he has invited to participate in numerous conferences, labs, seminars, etc. in other Universities, Conservatoires of Music, Film Schools, through Spain, as well as in Mexico. Author of two books of Film Music: Enciclopedia de las Bandas Sonoras (Ediciones B), Música de Cine: Una ilusión óptica (LibrosEnRed). He has also co-authored several collective books. Member of the Organizational Commitee of the International Film Music Festival in Ubeda, now the International Film Music Festival of Cordoba. As teacher, he has shared talks, classes and conferences with composers such as Michael Giacchino, Dave Grusin, Ludovic Bource, Bruno Coulais, Patrick Doyle, Mark Isham, Bruce Broughton, John Scott, Joel McNeely, Christopher Young, Wataru Hokoyama, Christopher Lennertz, Blake Neely, Bear McCreary, Lolita Ritmanis, Kristopher Carter, Michael McCuistion, Boris Slavov, Trevor Morris, Richard Bellis, as well as almost all Spanish composers of film music. He has interviewed many composers (Jerry Goldsmith, Ennio Morricone, Maurice Jarre, Pino Donaggio, Elmer Bernstein, Luis Bacalov, John Addison, etc) whose experiences and visions have being decisive in the creation of *The Music Script in Film*.

www.mundobso.com
cxa@mundobso.com
Twitter: @MundoBso